WRITING ABOUT LITERATURE

A GUIDE FOR STUDENTS

BENJAMIN G. FOSTER

Choate Rosemary Hall

Longman

NEW YORK

Consultants:

Joanne Lanouette
The Sidwell Friends School

Neil Mahoney
Scarsdale High School

Edwin Sundt
Landon School

Writing About Literature

Copyright © 1993 by Longman Publishing Group.
All rights reserved.
No part of this publication may be reproduced,
stored in a retrieval system, or transmitted
in any form or by any means, electronic, mechanical,
photocopying, recording, or otherwise,
without the prior permission of the publisher.

Longman, 10 Bank Street, White Plains, N.Y. 10606

Associated companies:
Longman Group Ltd., London
Longman Cheshire Pty., Melbourne
Longman Paul Pty., Auckland
Copp Clark Pitman, Toronto

Executive editor: Lyn McLean
Cover design: Joseph DePinho

ISBN 0-8013-0991-3

1 2 3 4 5 6 7 8 9 10-AL-9695949392

CONTENTS

PREFACE: TO THE TEACHER

LITERATURE-BASED WRITING

Most of us teaching English are drawn to our vocation through a love of literature. At the secondary level we typically create a curriculum that reflects this love and teach courses organized by their literary content. It is natural for teachers of such courses to assign writing that helps students to explore and understand the literature. Thus in many college-preparatory schools a literature-based writing program evolves from the primary purpose of teaching literature. This text has grown from a literature-based writing program at the Choate Rosemary Hall school and is designed to help students write on works such as Dickens' *Great Expectations*, Twain's *Adventures of Huckleberry Finn*, Zora Hurston's *Their Eyes Were Watching God*, Sophocles'' *Oedipus Rex*, Shakespeare's *Hamlet*, and the poetry of Shakespeare, Dickinson, and Yeats, to mention just a few of the authors and titles discussed in these pages. I hope that this indication of some of the literature discussed here suggests the levels appropriate for this text.

PROCESS WRITING

I have used as the basic organizing principle of this text the writing procedures and activities called *process writing*. Process writing emphasizes the stages of producing a paper: the ways students can begin with notes, jot lists, journal entries, brainstorming, and other rough beginnings and move through drafts and revisions to finished papers. Process writing has brought to the classroom a focus on the procedures that professional writers and editors use in preparing a text, and it has helped us to see more clearly the roles of the note-taker, the creative scribbler, the organizer, the critic, and the copy editor who live at least in potential form in all writers. There is no doubt that students need our help in developing these roles. Without our help, most of them conceive of writing as an exercise in which the writer sits at a desk and produces a final draft in a single session. By contrast, professional writers concentrate their efforts on prewriting and revising. In a recent study, professional writers were found to spend over 80 percent of their time engaged in prewriting, less than 5 percent in creating the first draft, and approximately 15 percent in revising. Process writing encourages all of us, teachers and students alike, to model our writing procedures on this professional approach.

COMPUTERS & PROCESS WRITING

The teaching of process writing has been greatly helped by computers. Tasks students once looked on with dread, such as formatting and cutting and pasting, turn out to be easy if not enjoyable on a computer. The ease of revision on a computer has encouraged many teachers to focus more on this stage of writing and to require more revisions from their students. The word *rewrite* penned in red ink on a student paper does not arouse the same resistance when the student has the paper on a computer disk. In this text I have pointed to the ways that students can use the resources of computers for each stage of the writing process.

THE FIVE-PARAGRAPH ESSAY

I have limited my emphasis on the widely used five-paragraph essay as the model for development. Increasingly the five-paragraph essay has aroused questions and doubts among English teachers. Some critics see it as a straight jacket, and many teachers find it too mechanical and predictable. Aren't there more authentic ways for students to respond to literature? I have attempted to show several models for development of the critical essay, and I have drawn from student writing that ranges from single-paragraph responses in a journal to lengthy arguments worked out in more than five paragraphs. Nor have I insisted on the five-paragraph essay's formulaic introductory and closing paragraphs. It is in these opening and closing paragraphs that the five-paragraph essay diverges most widely from the actual practice of professional writers.

Other teachers of college-bound secondary school students have questioned the supreme value placed on the formal critical paper no matter what its organizing principle or number of paragraphs. Is the graduate school model of the formal thesis paper the best one for secondary students? Should teachers insist that students come up with a thesis in order to write something meaningful on a text? Clearly we needn't reduce all student writing on literature to thesis defense. Other critics point out the narrowness imposed on student writing when we use it primarily as a test to determine whether our students have done their reading and come up with the "correct" view of the assigned text. They question the heavy emphasis on the formal critical paper at the secondary level. In agreement with this criticism, I have suggested alternative assignments, such as the personal responses of journals and the exploratory writing of response papers.

Finally I hope that, by presenting at length the writing of students who have been excited by literature, I can shift the focus away from process toward the literature and toward authentic and enthusiastic responses from our students. We come to our profession through our love of literature; isn't this what we most wish to inspire in our students? Aren't we eager for them to develop their own fresh and imaginative responses, no matter what form or length they take? If this text can in some small way help students to articulate their authentic responses in a coherent form, then it will serve its purpose.

INTRODUCTION: TO THE STUDENT

WHY CRITICAL WRITING?

This text focuses primarily on the writing of critical papers. Students of English often ask their teachers, "Why must we write critical papers?" It's a legitimate question, one concerned with purposes and values. It's a question that implies another: "What does the writing of critical papers teach that is important to us?"

An answer to this question was suggested by the comments of the admissions director at one of the Ivy League's most venerable law schools when he explained why he advises future law students to study liberal arts. The liberal arts, he pointed out, prepare students to read texts critically. The study of subjects such as history and literature sharpen students' abilities to follow passages of closely reasoned argument, to summarize the argument in their own words, to evaluate its worth, and to write a defense or a critique of the argument. These are precisely the skills needed in the study and practice of law. One might add that they are the skills needed in the study and practice of many of the professions. They are the skills taught preeminently by critical reading and writing.

CRITICAL READING AND CRITICAL WRITING

It is helpful to associate critical reading with critical writing and see them as two stages of a single act. No one can write valuable critical commentary on a work of literature who has not first read that work critically. Critical reading is close reading. Critical reading occurs when the student opens the book with a pen in hand, underlines key words, lines, and passages, makes notes and comments in the margins, and raises questions. It occurs when the student takes the time to examine the text to discover its basic argument and the way that argument is organized and worded. Critical reading means studying a text rather than skimming it for plot or information. It means reading with focused attention.

Critical writing takes critical reading a step further. It is valuable because it engages the student in a dialogue with the author, drawing the student into a productive relationship with the text. Serious reading honors the words of the author and work of literature, and critical writing develops this appreciative activity. Serious reading says that this text—be it Shakespeare's *Hamlet* or Hurston's *Their Eyes Were Watching God,* or Yeats' "The Second Coming"—has something important to say to me, and I want to explore what that something is; I want to dig deep in this work to discover everything I can in it that speaks to me and for me. One of the best ways to dig deep into a work of literature is through our own writing. We write about Hamlet to find out what he has to say to us. We voice our insights into Hamlet's problem in our own words because by doing so we help to discover what that problem is and how it relates to our lives.

Students often complain that critical writing is too difficult for them, too intellectual, too logical and dry. Yes, it is difficult. And yes, it does demand that students use their minds and sharpen their use of logic and the other intellectual tools that make for good analysis—the ability to make distinctions, for example, or the ability to compare and contrast two characters or two styles, or the ability to define terms precisely and to squeeze the essence of an argument from a text. But it is important to notice that these abilities are central to much education and to many of the world's professions (as the law-school admissions dean reminded us). The very fact that these are difficult intellectual tasks argues in favor of critical writing. It is a way of learning these skills—a part of the process of writing to learn as well as learning to write.

Writing to learn means writing to think. We write in order to bring the airy stuff of the brain down to earth, to make our thoughts solid and visible. William Butler Yeats' poem, "Balloon of the Mind," speaks to this process:

> Hands, do what you're bid:
> Bring the balloon of the mind
> That bellies and drags in the wind
> Into its narrow shed.

We put pen to paper or tap on a keyboard to bring "the balloon of the mind" down to earth "into its narrow shed." When we write we can see our thoughts take visible form. How can we know what we think unless we engage in the struggle to put our thoughts down on paper or on the computer screen? When we write, we do more than record our ideas, we generate ideas. We become creative. The critical writer is also a creative writer and a creative thinker. This, then, can be a value of writing papers about literature: that through them we learn to think about literature and thus learn to think about life and about ourselves. What could be a more worthwhile challenge than this?

THE WRITING PROCESS: AN OVERVIEW

COMPOSING THE PAPER

Gathering Information
- close reading and note-taking
- interpreting the text
- taking notes in class
- consulting secondary sources

Coming Up with Ideas
- journals
- jot lists
- brainstorming
- free writing
- clustering

Defining Audience & Purpose

Defining Topic & Thesis
- limiting topic
- turning topic into thesis
- supporting thesis

Using Quotations
- quotations as the foundation of writing
- length of quotations
- setting quotations into text
- documenting quotations

Organizing & Outlining

Writing the Rough Draft
- rapid writing
- building paragraphs
- introductions
- conclusions

EDITING, REVISING, & REWRITING THE PAPER

Editing
- writer as editor
- peer editors

Revising
- revising content, logic, and structure
- revising grammar, words, and sentences
- cutting and pasting

Writing the Final Draft
- final proofreading
- formatting

1

FIRST STEPS: PREWRITING

- **The Challenge of Critical Writing**
- **The Need for Detailed Knowledge**
- **Close Reading**
- **Interpreting the Text**
- **Taking Notes in Class**
- **Consulting Secondary Sources**
- **Using a Computer for Taking Notes**
- **Prewriting Illustrated: Student Notes & Paper**
- **Avoiding Commercial Study Guides**

THE CHALLENGE OF CRITICAL WRITING

The Problem of Beginnings

If you are like many students setting out to write a paper about literature, you may discover the truth of an insight from the British poet Lord Byron. "Nothing," he wrote, "is so difficult as a beginning." You may find that the words most difficult to put on paper are those you want to open your discussion. You sit down to write with high hopes of opening your paper with a burst of brilliance, but the words refuse to cooperate. You have hardly begun, and already you feel blocked.

Before you began writing you felt that you had some wonderful ideas, but now they resist your efforts to put them into words. The few ideas you manage to pin to the page turn out to be less inspiring than they seemed when they were floating around in your head. On paper they strike you as dull and unproductive. Other bright insights have evaporated. Where did they go? Why are these papers about literature so difficult to write?

1

Prewriting as the First Step

The problem many students face as they launch themselves into the first draft of a literary essay amounts to a leap over the first steps. A first or rough draft should not begin the writing process. Before writing a first draft, professional writers typically have done much of their work. This preparatory work has come to be labeled *prewriting*. Students can gain some of the mastery of professional writers if they recognize the value of prewriting and incorporate its steps in a formal and deliberate way into their writing procedures. According to one study of the habits of writers, professional writers spend over 80 percent of their working time on prewriting, less than 5 percent composing a rough draft, and about 15 percent revising and editing. By contrast, student writers often omit the steps of prewriting altogether or rush through them with little recognition of their value.

THE NEED FOR DETAILED KNOWLEDGE

You take an important first step in writing papers about literature when you recognize that they are difficult to write because they depend on a detailed understanding of the literature you are assigned to discuss. The prewriting that is a crucial step in all writing includes in literary papers the close reading, note-taking, and interpretation that precede the drafting of the paper. Your inspiration, creativity, and verbal abilities that can often carry you through personal and creative writing cannot pull off the same feat when you are asked to write on the role of Pearl in Nathaniel Hawthorne's *The Scarlet Letter* or the nature of the ghost in William Shakespeare's *Hamlet*. A literary paper requires information, insights, ideas, and judgments beyond those demanded by many other kinds of writing. The understanding of the literature that is a prerequisite for an informative critical paper poses problems especially when you must write about works like *Hamlet* or *The Scarlet Letter*, literature that is dense, subtle, and challenging.

You must meet the demand for detailed knowledge head on. There is no way around it. Once you gain the concrete information and detailed understanding needed—names of characters, who says what to whom, how and why the characters behave as they do, where and when specific actions take place, what language the author uses and why, and other similar considerations—and have written this information down, you have made a good beginning and have moved on your way to writing valuable literary commentary.

Beginning with a Wealth of Information

You increase your own confidence in writing if you start out armed with a wealth of information. Assemble written facts in surplus—the dates of the author's life and of the work under consideration, the historical background of the work, and anything else that might bear on your topic. More important for most literary papers than biographical and historical information are your insights and observations. Your understanding of the ways Huck Finn differs from Tom Sawyer in social status, ways of acting, and styles of speaking can be termed facts for a literary paper that compares the two. The more time you invest in gathering such facts, the more you will find that the task of putting words on paper flows from your information.

CLOSE READING

The Importance of Good Study Conditions

Informative papers grow from close reading. Close reading means study and depends on establishing a helpful working environment for your reading. Insist on quiet. Work at a desk. Develop the habit of reading with pen in hand. Reading at a desk with pen in hand is obviously a less relaxed way to work than sitting on your bed with music playing, but it allows you to make notes and to write down insights and ideas easily. Furthermore, it announces that you are at work, which brings with it the psychological advantage of intensity.

Taking Notes on the Text

Make marginal notes in your text. If you prefer to keep your text clean, make your notes on slips of paper that you can slide into the text. Put the title of the work and the page number on these slips, since they have a way of escaping from the pages where they belong. Make these notes before class while you are first reading the text. Include questions; these can remind you of passages, word use, and ideas you did not understand during your reading that you want to discuss in class. Write as well questions that may be valuable for discussion. Underline passages you find important, adding marginal comments on their significance.

INTERPRETING THE TEXT

When you take notes in the margins of your text and underline passages, you have begun to interpret the text. At the simplest level, interpretation involves deciding what is important, what passages to underline, what is central to the text. It means coming up with basic questions about the text, questions such as the following: Who are the main characters? What are their concerns and interests? What is the author's attitude toward the characters? What does the author gain by the style of this work? What would be gained or lost if the story or poem were written in some other way? Is there is a major conflict? If there is a major conflict, then who is struggling against whom? What does this struggle represent?

These are questions about characters, style, and plot. Questions such as these plus a host of others should come to you immediately as you read. To turn to a specific example, as you make your way with Huck and Jim on the raft down the Mississippi in Mark Twain's *The Adventures of Huckleberry Finn*, you may wonder about the differences in the characters and the ways these differences color their views of what is happening around them. Huck and Jim express opinions on the origins of the stars, the peacefulness of the river, the threat of the shore towns, and their hopes for freedom. How do their ideas differ? In what ways can the differences in their ideas and attitudes be attributed to the differences in their backgrounds? These are of course elementary questions, but even the most basic questions are valuable means of entering the text and can lead to interpretation. If you write down your questions as you read, not only will you deepen your understanding of the text, but you will also begin to assemble the materials that may lead to a paper.

Let us assume that at the end of your reading you will be writing a paper on *The Adventures of Huckleberry Finn*. Looking through your text for a topic, you come upon your questions about Huck and Jim and feel that these might lead you to a closer study of the two characters. After reviewing your text and your notes, you feel drawn to examine how each one views the concept of freedom. As you make your investigations into the text and ask further questions, you come up with the idea of a comparison and contrast paper on the views of an older black man running from slavery with a young white boy running from home. Thus the first steps of interpretation will have led you to a topic and a way of organizing it, which in turn will lead you to further interpretation that can yield the information, ideas, and judgments that make up literary papers.

TAKING NOTES IN CLASS

During class on the assigned text, follow the discussion with your text open, adding to your reading notes and underlining passages that your teacher and classmates have discussed. Frequently the papers you write grow from class discussions, and if you use class time productively you may find that your teacher and classmates have contributed information and insights that can move you forward in your writing. Especially if you have been preparing for classes by reading closely and taking notes, you will find that you have already begun the information-gathering process.

One caution may be in order in this context. Many teachers want you to come up with original insights and a fresh point of view in your literary papers. They may penalize you for drawing too heavily on class discussion. Yet even if you are asked to produce a paper with fresh ideas, you may be stimulated to come up with original insights by recording the thoughts of your teacher and classmates. Use the ideas of others as a challenge to come up with your own. The creation of original ideas can be a dialectical process set in motion by the commentary of your teacher and classmates and sharpened by your note-taking.

In addition to recording your teacher's comments and your classmates' observations during class, try writing a summary of class discussion when the class is over. Add your own responses to this summary so that you continue to sharpen the dialectic process. This frequent recording and digesting of information and observations develops your writing abilities as it provides you with information and insights for your papers.

CONSULTING SECONDARY SOURCES

Using Library Materials

Although your own insights and ideas usually provide the chief sources for your literary papers, secondary sources can be helpful for certain papers. *Secondary sources* are books and articles in reference works and periodicals and other documents typically found in a library that provide information about the literary work you are studying, which can be called the *primary text*. (The research paper, which draws heavily from a variety of secondary sources, is a different kind of work from the literary papers discussed here.) The primary text is usually a book you own, but secondary materials most often belong to a library, and they must be treated differently from your own books. You should not underline in library books and magazines nor make marginal notes in them.

Taking Abundant Notes on Secondary Sources

Other important differences separate the way you go about gathering information from secondary sources from the way you treat the primary text. If you are required to use the secondary sources in the library, you will need to take more abundant notes on them. Furthermore, probably not all of the article or book you consult as a secondary source will be relevant to your topic, and you will need to skim chapters and passages to find the pertinent portions. You will also want to write down a number of direct quotations from your secondary sources since you may not have the work handy as you write. For the same reason you must be precise in recording page numbers and the publication information (e.g., author's full name, title and edition of the work, publication place and date), which you will need to document your sources when you come to write your paper.

Note Cards & Half-Sheets

For note-taking from secondary sources, many teachers recommend the use of note cards or half-sheets, and these are often handy for notes on your primary text. You may find that 3 x 5 inch note cards work better than a notebook because they can be assembled and reassembled in different ways as you proceed on your paper. Some writers find these cards too small; unless your handwriting is tiny, you cannot fit much on a card. Others like the brevity that they enforce.

If you find note cards too cramped, try half-sheets, 5 x 8 inch sheets that can be organized with topic headings and arranged in the same way as note cards. Note cards or a collection of half-sheets work especially well for literary papers because you can title them with acts, scenes, chapters, stanzas, and the other divisions in the literature. Then you can organize your paper by organizing the cards or sheets.

USING A COMPUTER FOR TAKING NOTES

Electronic Notepad & Scrapbook

A computer is an excellent tool for note-taking when you work with primary or secondary sources. Many writing programs for computers supply you with an electronic notepad or scrapbook where you can file notes and quotations. You can paste these materials directly into your text when you want them, or you can cut material from your paper and save it in the scrapbook or notepad as you work on your paper.

Perhaps the easiest way to take notes on a computer is to create a file with an appropriate title—the title of the work of literature on which you are working, for example, or the title of your paper—and record there the quotations and notes you want to introduce into your paper. The file becomes the equivalent of a notebook or of note cards. If your collection of notes and quotations is lengthy, you will be unable to see everything in your computer file at once. In such cases print out the file before you begin writing a draft of your paper.

Using Computer Notes

Notes and quotations gathered in a computer file are easily edited and moved, and thus the use of a computer for note-taking brings benefits for organizing. When you finish gathering your materials in the scrapbook or notebook, scroll through your file and look for ways to group your notes and quotations under headings. Put the headings in bold print. These headings can become the major divisions of an outline.

Gathering Quotations in a File

Include in your file or on your note cards more quotations than you think you will use. It is helpful to have a choice of quotations when you come to writing the paper. In this, as in gathering the other information that creates a literary paper, you want to accumulate your materials in abundance. When you write your paper it will be an easy task to copy the quotations from your file and paste them into your paper. Add to your file your commentaries on these quotations and your notes on the secondary sources. These are easily transferred to your paper. The ease with which notes, comments, and quotations can be put on file and then moved from one place to another recommends a computer as part of the prewriting of a literary paper.

PREWRITING ILLUSTRATED: STUDENT NOTES & PAPER ON ZORA NEALE HURSTON'S *THEIR EYES WERE WATCHING GOD*

Prewriting Step 1: Close Reading & Note-Taking

Below are the notes a student took in her text as she prepared for a class discussion of Chapter 2 of *Their Eyes Were Watching God*. Her teacher had asked the class to focus on the following topic, to serve as the basis first for a discussion in class and then for a two to three page paper to be written outside of class.

> Topic: "Write on Janie's conception of love and marriage. You might compare her conception with her grandmother's views."

In Chapter 2 of this novel, Janie, the central character, lies beneath a pear tree and has a vision of sensual beauty and fertility. The student recognized that the chapter presented Janie's vision of love, which deserved consideration in the student's paper. Here is the paragraph describing that vision, along with the student's notes on the text:

sanctum: "a sacred place"

calyx: "the outer whorl of protective leaves of a flower"

> She was stretched on her back beneath the pear tree soaking in the alto chant of the visiting bees, the gold of the sun and the panting breath of the breeze when the inaudible voice of it all came to her. She saw a dust-bearing bee sink into the <u>sanctum</u> of a bloom; the thousand sister-<u>calyxes</u> arch to meet the love embrace and the ecstatic shiver of the tree from root to tiniest branch creaming in every blossom and frothing with delight. <u>So this was a marriage!</u> She had been summoned to behold a revelation. Then Janie felt a pain remorseless sweet that left her limp and <u>languid.</u>

Janie's vision of marriage comes from a pear tree in bloom — close to nature

languid: "without vigor; drooping"

Religious words like sanctum combined with inspiration from nature: religious view of nature? of marriage? View of nature & marriage very romantic. Adolescent view. Janie eager to marry?

Two paragraphs after the vision of the pear tree in *Their Eyes Were Watching God* occurs the following passage, included here with the student's notes:

Johnny Taylor — her first romantic interest?

shiftless: "lacking the will or ability to do or accomplish; lazy"

> Through the pollinated air she saw a <u>glorious being</u> coming up the road. In her former blindness she had known him as <u>shiftless Johnny Taylor</u>, tall and lean. That was before the <u>golden dust</u> of pollen had <u>beglamored</u> his rags and her eyes.

"glorious being" "golden dust" "beglamored" } *vision beneath pear tree transforms Janie's view of men*

Distorted view of Johnny Taylor? Janie too romantic? Nanny's views of men more realistic?

As these notes indicate, the student was not certain if the reader was meant to admire Janie's highly romantic vision of marriage gained beneath the blossoming pear tree. It seemed to this student that perhaps the grandmother's view of life was the more realistic and mature, and that a comparison of the two views should indicate that the older woman's view was ultimately more valuable and that Janie should grow up out of her adolescent and overly romantic view of the relationship between the sexes. But the student was not entirely comfortable with this conclusion, and she looked forward to class discussion as a way of clarifying her judgment.

Prewriting Step 2: Class Discussion & Notes

In class during discussion of *Their Eyes Were Watching God* the student added the following notes:

Class Notes on <u>Their Eyes Were Watching God</u>

Janie's Vision beneath pear tree - Moment of insight. sensual language charged with sexual energy. Coming of puberty and sexual maturity in Janie. New way of seeing males. Makes Johnny attractive.

Nanny: sees danger where Janie sees romance. Nanny made nervous because Janie has reached puberty and has interest in boys. Two opposing views of love & marriage:
Janie: sensual pleasure, romance.
Nanny: economic security.
Which view is right? Are both views equally valid?

The student's notes end with a question because the class ended with the same uncertainty. At the end of 50 minutes of discussion, the teacher and the students had not come up with any definitive answers. The teacher suggested that the students continue to explore this issue in their papers. To help them in their exploration, the teacher put on reserve in the library a secondary source, *Zora Neale Hurston: A Literary Biography*, by Robert E. Hemenway, and suggested they read especially Chapter 9, "Crayon Enlargements of Life."

Prewriting Step 3: Notes on Secondary Sources

The student was able to use a computer while studying the literary biography, and she wrote the following quotations and saved them in a file she named with the title of the novel. Of course the same notes could be taken by hand and filed in a notebook or on note cards.

STUDENT COMPUTER NOTES

Janie "raised by her grandmother to 'take a stand on high ground' and be spared the traditional fate reserved for black women as beasts of burden." page 232

Janie's love for Tea Cake: "Without the hypocrisy and the role-playing that characterized her other marriages, this love is strong enough to make both parties open and giving." page 233

"Hurston identifies Janie with a blossoming pear tree . . . the tree seems to represent the mystery of the springtime universe." page 233

Vision of the pear tree "comes to represent the organic union Janie searches for throughout her life." page 233

"She tells Joe that 'in some way we ain't natural wid one'nother.' Later, with Tea Cake, Janie feels in tune with natural process, just as she did under the pear tree as a child." page 234

"Her childhood had ended when a neighbor boy failed to fulfill her romantic dreams. Killicks initiated her further, showing that 'marriage did not make love. Janie's first dream was dead. So she became a woman.' ... Joe was a false dream too, 'just something she had grabbed up to drape her dreams over.' It is not until Tea Cake that her dream—now toughened by knowledge—can become truth." page 235

Notice that these notes are almost entirely quotations from the literary biography. There is no plan to the collection of quotations; they are simply recorded in the order that the student came to them. Later the student organized the quotations according to the plan of her paper. She cut them and pasted them into her text so that she did not need to copy them over again— one of the ways computers save time and the bother of copy-work. There are more quotations than the student will use, for she is working with the idea of gathering an abundance of information.

Formulating & Supporting a Thesis

After gathering the notes from the secondary source and reflecting on her reading about *Their Eyes Were Watching God*, the student decided that Janie's vision of love and marriage gained under the flowering pear tree was the right one, at least for her, and that Nannie's advice and direction betrayed Janie in important ways. She wrote the following thesis on her computer screen:

Thesis: Janie's conception of love gained under the pear tree is the guiding principle of her life.

The student planned to use this thesis as the starting point of her paper and also as the focus for its development. Notice that she has moved rapidly from her close reading and interpretation of the text, class discussion, and use of secondary sources to a thesis. Furthermore, much of the support for the thesis is already in her computer file in the form of quotations from the literary biography of Hurston. Her careful study and thoughtful approach have yielded several benefits in the form of short-cuts, and she does not need to labor over the tasks of generating ideas or formulating a thesis and then digging out support for her thesis. (These topics will be discussed in greater detail in the pages following.) Thus she has compressed into one or two steps the work that often requires several separate steps. This ease of coming up with a thesis and the ideas to support it are a credit to the student's close reading, that most essential prewriting step when writing about literature.

Creating an Organizational Plan

It is worth noting that the student's assignment had already provided the topic—Janie's conception of love and marriage—and pointed her in a certain direction in the suggestion that this conception be compared with the grandmother's views. The student followed this suggestion by writing a comparison and contrast paper. Thus the organizational plan was built into the topic, which is frequently the case with literary topics. Either something intrinsic in the topic calls for a certain approach, such as a comparison and contrast, or your teacher may assign the topic in a form that dictates an organizational plan. The final version of the paper in its entirety follows:

STUDENT PAPER

Janie's Romantic Views of Love & Marriage

In Zora Neale Hurston's novel *Their Eyes Were Watching God*, Janie has a vision of love as she lies under a flowering pear tree when she is sixteen years old. This vision is the most important event in her life because it provides a guiding principle that will direct the rest of her years. According to Robert E. Hemenway in *Zora Neale Hurston: A Literary Biography*, this vision of the pear tree "comes to represent the organic union Janie searches for throughout her life" (233). This vision defines the meaning of love and marriage for her.

She was stretched on her back beneath the pear tree soaking in the alto chant of the visiting bees, the gold of the sun and the panting breath of the breeze when the inaudible voice of it all came to her. She saw a dust-bearing bee sink into the sanctum of a bloom; the thousand sister-calyxes arch to meet the love embrace and the ecstatic shiver of the tree from root to tiniest branch creaming in every blossom and frothing with delight. So this was a marriage! She had been summoned to behold a revelation. Then Janie felt a pain remorseless sweet that left her limp and languid. (10, 11)

This vision of what is a good marriage is very romantic, but it is the best guiding vision for Janie. The author calls it a "revelation," implying it has a religious truth to it. The novel shows that when Janie marries according to some other guiding principle, she is not happy and fulfilled. For example, she first marries Logan Killicks, and she realizes quickly that he does not fulfill her vision of the right kind of marriage for her. After Janie marries Logan, she "went inside to wait for love to begin" (21), but it never does. She goes to Nanny, her grandmother, who has raised her and forced her to marry Logan, and complains about the marriage: "You told me Ah mus gointer love him, and, and Ah don't" (22). Soon she is disillusioned by her marriage. "She knew now that marriage did not make love. Janie's first dream was dead, so she became a woman" (24).

Janie's grandmother arranges the marriage with Logan because she wants Janie to have economic security. " 'Tain't Logan Killicks Ah wants you to have, baby, it's protection" (14). Because Logan owns land and has a reliable income, he can provide Janie with the economic necessities of life so that Janie won't be abused as a work animal or mule. Nanny's ideas about marriage are the opposite of Janie's, and she doesn't trust Janie's romantic views. She believes that marriage comes first and then love should grow from the marriage, but the novel shows that this doesn't happen for Janie. Nanny's vision of marriage is very practical. It lacks the idealism of Janie's vision, and, even though it could be called realistic, it still isn't the best vision for Janie, who is romantic at heart and needs a romantic marriage to find fulfillment. According to Hemenway, Janie's marriage to Logan Killicks was characterized by "hypocrisy" and "role-playing" (233), showing that without romance marriage isn't authentic for Janie.

After a second marriage to a wealthy businessman which also is false, Janie finally meets Tea Cake, a man who does fulfill her vision of a romantic relationship. Nanny is no longer alive, but if she were she would not approve of this relationship, because Tea Cake is somewhat irresponsible and does not provide the economic security that Nanny wanted for her grandchild. But for Janie, Tea Cake is the answer to her longings. In the words of Hemenway, "Later, with Tea Cake, Janie feels in tune with natural process, just as she did under the pear tree as a child" (234).

The novel shows at the end a picture of Janie fulfilled in her romantic longings. It proves that Janie's idealistic vision is also realistic and something she can live by, and, even though Tea Cake dies and Janie ends in mourning, she knows that her early vision is true, and she has many happy memories with which to live. "Ah done been tuh de horizon and back and now Ah kin set heah in mah house and live by comparisons," she says to her friend, Pheoby, in the final pages of the novel. "Dis house ain't so absent of things lak it used tuh be befo' Tea Cake come along. It's full uh thoughts, 'specially dat bedroom."

Janie ends up without the economic security her grandmother wanted for her, but she has something more important. She has lived a fulfilled life, and she has a rich supply of memories.

The paper represents in part the fruits of prewriting, especially of close reading, note-taking, and the study of a secondary source. The student felt that once she had assembled the quotations from the novel and the secondary source, the paper "wrote itself," which is a frequent comment of students who have invested a generous amount of time in prewriting. Notice how frequently the student uses relevant quotations from the novel. Frequent use of apt quotations is often a sign of close textual study. This frequent use of Hurston's language helps to keep the student writer close to the text she is exploring while it helps the reader of the paper to gain some of the flavor of the novel.

AVOIDING COMMERCIAL STUDY GUIDES

Although the student wrote the paper above on *Their Eyes Were Watching God* with the help of her classmates, teacher, and secondary sources, the paper is clearly hers. It advances her thesis, and the thesis is supported by quotations she has dug from her own reading of the novel and the critical biography. The student worked from a close relationship to the texts, and she used her writing to explore her understanding of the novel as well as to develop her views and deepen her insights.

By contrast, a paper based on a hasty reading of the novel supplemented by a commercial study guide does not provide an opportunity to explore the literature and to develop your own ideas. Commercial study guides do not offer a worthwhile substitute for reading and understanding the literary work. The knowledge of a literary work that guides you is vague, generalized summary that fails to equip you for writing. If you use a commercial guide as a substitute for the literature, you rob yourself of any chance to get inside the work, understand the characters, and savor the language. Papers based on commercial study guides suffer from a secondhand quality. Such papers typically are thin, sketchy, and lacking in any personal flavor. In reading them, teachers can usually detect that the student has not read the work. Many teachers and many schools consider the use of commercial study guides to constitute plagiarism.

2

COMING UP WITH IDEAS

- **Journals**
- **Jot Lists**
- **Brainstorming**
- **Freewriting**
- **Clustering**
- **Secondary Sources**

THE IMPORTANCE OF IDEAS

"All there is to writing is having ideas," the poet Robert Frost said. "To learn to write is to learn to have ideas." These words should not suggest that writing is simple, as if coming up with ideas is easy or that once you have them the rest of the task follows with little effort. It's no small matter to come up with valuable ideas about a work of literature, ideas that are fresh and original, rooted closely in the text, and productive of further reflection.

As Chapter 1 indicated, you take the primary step in prewriting for a paper on literature by studying the literary work closely. If things go well, then ideas will arise from this close study. They may arise as you sit alone at your desk, as you study the text in class with others, during discussion with a teacher or a classmate outside of class, or from consulting a secondary source. But if ideas do not come to you from these sources, what can you do? Are there techniques for generating ideas that apply to literary writing?

Fortunately the answer is yes. Writers and teachers of writing have spent considerable time on this problem of coming up with ideas, and several techniques have been developed to help student writers generate ideas. All of these techniques are part of prewriting; they precede the writing of the first draft. If used effectively, they can make the writing of the first draft flow naturally from the materials you have assembled.

JOURNALS

Keeping a Reading Journal

Journals are an extension of the close reading and interpretation of the text discussed in Chapter 1. Sometimes called a reading journal to distinguish it from a personal journal, it provides an ideal way for you to respond to your reading. Use a journal to respond to a text immediately after you have finished your reading. The text should be fresh in your mind; you want to capture your immediate responses, the first impressions that often disappear if you don't record them. The journal then becomes a way to reflect on these immediate responses, cultivating your powers of reflection and thoughtfulness as well as your powers of observation.

Developing the Habit of Journal Writing

Journal writing grows in value as it becomes a habit. Try to establish the habit of writing in your journal at the end of each day's reading. Even if you spend no more than five or ten minutes jotting down a few sentences or phrases, the habit will carry you forward and provide you with an abundance of material in the long run. Don't worry that some of your journal entries seem uninspired or obvious. Keep working at your journal through the dull times as well as the moments of inspiration.

Informal Journal Style

Like a personal journal, a reading journal focuses on your personal responses, and when it works well it helps you to develop your own voice and style. As a rule, journal writers write from the first person, often in a relaxed and informal manner. If you are writing strictly for yourself, you can use whatever words, grammar, and tone arise at the moment—you are meeting no one's demands but your own. Often journals provide the only writing opportunity to enjoy this private and personal quality. It is intimate in ways that other writing is not. Thus it may seem very different from the composition of a literary paper that assumes a public, formal voice, yet journal writing can nourish our writing life in ways that benefit all our writing. It is a fact that most professional writers keep a journal and find it indispensable for cultivating their writing abilities.

If you are submitting your journal to your teacher and sharing your entries with your class, you still may be given considerable freedom in the writing. For example, your teacher may not demand a formal level of grammatical correctness and word choice in your journal entries. You may be free to use fragments or collections of phrases with minimal punctuation.

Notice how the following journal entry on the death of Ophelia written by a student when she finished reading Act IV of Shakespeare's *Hamlet* has an informal and relaxed quality expressed in part by the use of the first-person pronoun and by fragments:

STUDENT JOURNAL ENTRY

Poor Ophelia! So vulnerable, so defenseless! Somehow you know she is going to die young from the first. She has no defenses to allow her to make it in the world of political intrigue and treachery. I find it difficult to know what she is really like—she is always being used by others. By her father, for example. She is like a piece of bait Polonius uses to attract Hamlet so he can prove something to the king. Or earlier he delivers that sermon to beware of Hamlet and don't trust men. And all Ophelia does is say yes my lord. The dutiful daughter. And then Hamlet treats her so harshly in the "Get thee to a nunnery" scene. To me she seems entirely too passive. I keep wanting her to fight back, to tell Hamlet or her father to get off her case, let her live her life the way she wants to live it. I see her death as similar to her life—no effort, no fighting back, just passively floating along on the stream until she drowns. It's as if she can't even see she's in danger: "As one incapable of her own distress" is the way the queen describes it. Is this even suicide? It's like everything else in her life—it happens to her, she doesn't cause it to happen. To me she's the classic female victim from beginning to end. In describing her drowning, Shakespeare calls her "the poor wretch," maybe his way of stating something similar about her.

Anchoring Journal Writing to the Text with Quotations

This journal entry advances the student's personal responses and expresses her opinions while it anchors the discussion to the text, referring to specific scenes and actions and quoting from the speech that describes Ophelia's death. Thus it does two things that are hallmarks of much good writing on literature: It provides a point of view—that Ophelia is too passive and ends up as a victim—while it remains close to the literary work.

Journal Entries as Germs of Ideas for Papers

Later this student was able to enlarge on this point of view to write a fully developed paper on Ophelia as a female victim in a world run by men. Her journal entry provided her with a first step in composing this paper, and she found she could make use of her references to the play's actions (Ophelia's father's warning about Hamlet and use of her as bait and Hamlet's rejection of her) as steps in her paper's organization. In short, her journal entry was the germ of her paper, both in ideas and organization.

A series of journal entries on your reading provides an especially helpful resource of topics and ideas for literary papers. Let us say you study Shakespeare's *Hamlet* over the course of two weeks, faithfully recording your responses in your journal at the end of each reading. Your journal then becomes a storehouse of some eight or ten small essays on the play, each opening up the possibility of a larger development. When you must meet the challenge of a paper assignment, especially one for which you select the topic, you are at a considerable advantage over classmates who fail to keep any record of their responses to the reading.

Journals are one of the few techniques of prewriting that resist the use of a computer. There are some computer-happy students who write everything on a computer, including their journal entries, but most writers, including those wedded to computer technology, like the intimacy of taking pen in hand and writing in a special notebook or journal. If you feel like trying a computer for your journal, here are some suggestions from those who have been keeping electronic journals:

• Keep all of your journal entries pretty much as you wrote them on a given date. Don't edit and change them, because part of the value of journal entries is their record of what you thought and felt at a specific moment. The ease of editing on a computer may entice you into editing and improving your writing as you review your past entries, but unless you resist this urge, you risk destroying the freshness and value of your original entries. If you wish to add comments later, then date the additions so that you can distinguish your original responses from your later reflections.

• Print out your journal entries frequently—preferably each time you write one—and collect them in a notebook that you reserve strictly for your journal. Label it clearly. You want to have your journal handy for browsing and for review. You might then pen additional comments as you read through your material.

• Each time you add a new page, look back over your earlier entries. Journal writing, whether done on a computer or with pen and ink, is a process that encourages reflection and deepens your appreciation of literature as it enlarges your capacity for imaginative response to what you have read.

JOT LISTS

Lists provide an effective means to pin down fleeting ideas that might otherwise disappear. They are a quick way to record thoughts and to begin to organize your knowledge. Although lists are not formal outlines and may seem insubstantial and sketchy, their very sketchiness can work for you. A list provides a quick summary of facts and ideas and can generate more ideas. Used freely it becomes a device to tap into your mind's powers of free association. One word or phrase summons up an additional related word or phrase. Here, for example, is a jot list drawn up by a student assigned to write a brief paper on the setting of "The Lottery," the short story by Shirley Jackson:

STUDENT JOT LIST

> rural village of farming people
> maybe New England or Midwest
> time: June in early 20th century (tractors show it's fairly modern)
>
> men talk of planting and rain
> seasons important
> lottery associated with spring season and crops
> simple, uneducated people
> traditional ways followed without question
> close-knit community
> friendly people, know one another by name
> must be some hidden hatreds, suppressed violence

When the author of this list came to write his paper, he began with the final three items, which shows how an initial list is suggestive—a quick way to let the mind bring concepts to the surface and begin to articulate them. It also shows how a list can serve as a first step in organization as well as idea creation. Here is the paper in its entirety. (Notice that this is not a formal literary paper and so makes no use of documentation.)

STUDENT PAPER

The Violent Townspeople in Jackson's "The Lottery"

The rural village of Shirley Jackson's "The Lottery" may seem like a friendly place, but it's not. It's dangerous and violent. The people who live there know their neighbors' names and a lot of gossip about everyone, and they probably have all kinds of grudges and hatreds that aren't mentioned at first. That's what I concluded from the violence at the end. They all seem happy that the lottery victim is someone else, and they don't show any sympathy for Tessie Hutchinson, the woman they stone to death. The people in this farming town are basically violent, even though they cover up their violence with friendliness.

The story points out that these are traditional people who follow rituals. They don't seem to know why they do some of the things they do, such as using the black box. There's talk of making a new box, "but no one liked to upset even as much tradition as was represented by the black box." So they keep doing the same things in the same ways for years and years, like primitive people. They don't seem to have much education because they believe that the lottery helps the crops. This is a town of ignorant, traditional, violent people.

It's a tradition in this town to stone one of the townspeople to death every year, so they go ahead and do it, without asking questions. The worst one is Mr. Hutchinson, who "went over to his wife and forced the slip of paper out of her hand." Then he joins in throwing rocks. Maybe he cares for his wife and family in some way, but he also must have violent feelings against her, just like all of the other people in this town. It might look like a New England or Midwest farming village you'd see on a calendar, but watch out, because these people will kill you without even thinking about it.

It is easy to see that although the jot list was not used in its entirety, it provided much of the thinking that went into the paper along with the point of view that despite appearing friendly, the people in the town are dangerously violent. Thus the jot list, sketchy as it was, went a considerable distance in helping the student to write his paper.

Computer Jot Lists

Jot lists can be drawn up on a computer. Many of the techniques of prewriting lend themselves naturally to the use of a computer. Prewriting techniques emphasize the quick, the suggestive, the provisional; and a computer screen is the perfect place to record and see such work. If you draw up your jot list on a computer, then print a copy to keep beside you as you compose your draft.

BRAINSTORMING

Free Association

Drawing up jot lists can be considered one form of *brainstorming*, a technique for generating and developing ideas. Brainstorming lends itself to group sessions, working in pairs, or solitary writing. Essentially the term can be applied to any process of writing down words, phrases, ideas, sentences, or questions quickly without stopping to edit or reflect. It draws on the mind's powers of free association, whereby one word or concept summons up related words and concepts.

Brainstorming taps the spontaneous and intuitive sides of our minds and thus must be done with the mind on automatic, as it were—allowing the mind to think by itself without the negative judgments we so often render on our thinking. Free association must be allowed to be free. When you brainstorm, allow yourself to be mentally uninhibited.

Setting a Time Limit

It is helpful to set a time limit for a brainstorming session. Brief periods work best. For example, set your clock for 10 minutes and then turn to your paper and write continuously, rapidly, unselfconsciously for the full 10 minutes. Keep your pen moving; don't lift it from the page. Don't stop to look at the clock or gaze out the window. If you are good at the keyboard, use a computer. Some students find it helpful to dim the computer screen during a brainstorming session so that they are not tempted to stop and edit.

Resisting the Impulse to Edit

It is important to resist any temptation to stop and think or to stop and edit. Brainstorming is not reflective thinking. Reflective, critical thinking uses a different side of the brain from intuitive, creative thinking. You will draw on your powers of critical thinking when you examine your writing with editorial tools, but that comes later, when you have created the ideas and statements for reflection. The editorial response is a reflective one, and it brings brainstorming to a halt.

Don't worry about grammar. Don't stop to finish your thoughts or to write complete sentences. Jot down words, phrases, ideas, whatever comes to mind. Keep going, recording it all, and if you run out of ideas, keep moving the pen anyway, or go on tap-tap-tapping on the keyboard, writing nonsense if nothing else comes to mind. You will end up with stream-of-consciousness writing, much of it fragmentary and jumbled. Don't worry that most of what you write during brainstorming may be silly, obvious, or off the subject. When you go back over the materials you produced in your brainstorming session, you'll find the valuable ideas.

Brainstorming on the Computer

If you do your brainstorming on a computer, you might highlight the important ideas in bold before printing out the material. Or you might use a larger type size to distinguish the material that looks promising.

A productive way to brainstorm for literary ideas is to write at the top of the page or at the top of the computer screen a direct quotation from the literary work you are studying. The quotation should be short and to the point. It should encapsulate a key idea from the literary work, the idea that you will use to spin off other ideas in your brainstorming session. More important, it should bring to mind an image. Images are the primal stuff of literature; they awaken our imaginations and stir our minds to respond.

Here are the results of one student's five-minute brainstorming session on Shakespeare's character Lady Macbeth. Working on a computer, he first typed at the top of the screen the words spoken by the sleepwalking Lady Macbeth, "All the perfumes of Arabia will not sweeten this little hand." He highlighted the quotation in bold. Then he began typing whatever came to mind as rapidly as he could. The student used no punctuation during the session, but left spaces between phrases. Afterward he went back and added dashes to separate the phrases.

STUDENT BRAINSTORMING

"All the perfumes of Arabia will not sweeten this little hand"

Sleepwalking at night —feels guilty—no way to get rid of guilt—earlier believed a little water would get rid of the blood—so now a new realism, new awareness of moral realities—shows her deep buried conscience—she's buried it during the earlier action—her subconscious mind at work—surprising side of this woman—earlier she seemed without morals, had no conscience—does her husband know about this side of her?—she doesn't even know herself—lonely, isolated individual in great pain—focus on her hand as part of her that asserts her will and takes action—now it needs to be sweetened—not a woman we associate with perfumes or other feminine things—she's been tough and political—she has operated with tough exterior in man's world of power politics—now her repressed feminine side coming out in her sleepwalking—she's like someone haunted—haunted by her lost feminine side—

From Chaos to Creation

You might ask, "Can anything valuable come out of this chaos?" Classical myth tells us that chaos precedes creation and is the stuff from which creation is shaped. Brainstorming techniques can be seen as ways to dredge from the mind the chaos that contains the raw material to be worked on to create something ordered and meaningful.

The author of the brainstorming session on Lady Macbeth found in his chaotic materials three ideas that he wanted to develop further:

1. Lady Macbeth had spent the early part of the play's action involved in the tough, masculine world of power politics.

2. Lady Macbeth had repressed her feminine side which she now associates with the perfumes of Arabia she wants to sweeten her hand.

3. Lady Macbeth's feminine side which she had repressed includes her moral conscience, which now comes back to haunt her.

The student highlighted the phrases that expressed these ideas in bold and printed out the sheet so that he had it handy as he worked on organizing his paper. For his next step he cut away the material he found irrelevant. He numbered the remaining phrases to suggest a sequence and an organizing plan. Printed out, this edited and organized version of his brainstorming materials looked like this:

STUDENT BRAINSTORMING ORGANIZED

"All the perfumes of Arabia will not sweeten this little hand"

1. not a woman we associate with perfumes or other feminine things—she's been tough and political—she has operated with tough exterior in man's world of power politics—she seemed without morals, had no conscience—
2. now her repressed feminine side coming out in her sleepwalking—she's like someone haunted—haunted by her lost feminine side—
3. feels guilty—shows her deep buried conscience—she's buried it during the earlier action—

Notice that this material comprises simply the phrases from the original brainstorming rearranged and numbered. On the computer it took only a couple of minutes of cutting and pasting to transform the original chaotic materials of the brainstorming session into a first rough outline that indicates the organization and some of the content of the paper. Using this outline, the student found that his writing was on the threshold of a rough draft. It required only another 25 or 30 minutes to rough out a draft based on this brainstorming. He found that the draft flowed easily in part because he wrote it immediately after the brainstorming session while its materials were still lively in his mind.

FREEWRITING

Another of the brainstorming techniques, freewriting is a timed exercise that draws on the mind's powers of free association. Freewriting taps into the flow of the mind and produces stream-of-consciousness writing. As in using any of the prewriting techniques aimed at creating the preliminary chaotic stuff of composition, it is crucial to keep writing no matter what comes up. There should be no reflection, no editing, no stopping. Set your time limit in advance—10 or 15 minutes, a short session—and keep writing for the full time even if you end up writing drivel.

In the following example of freewriting, the student was assigned to compare and contrast Hamlet and Laertes in Shakespeare's play. He used a computer for his freewriting and found it useful to dim the screen so that he would not be tempted to look back over his writing. Before he began his freewriting session he reread the scenes in acts iv and v where Laertes is important. Here are the results:

STUDENT FREEWRITING

Hamlet & Laertes

Laertes is a hothead. He acts without thinking. He acts like a bull in a china shop. In Act IV he rushes into the king and yells O thou vile king give me my father. He wants to usurp the king and take over the throne. Total hothead doesn't think just acts out of impulse. Never stops to consider the consequences of what he's doing but just rushes off to do it. Hamlet the opposite. You cannot picture Hamlet rushing into the king and confronting him directly. He's never direct. Hamlet does everything in a sly, indirect manner. He plays games and plays roles. He delays taking action to consider the consequences. So Hamlet is a man of thought compared to Laertes the man of action. Though Hamlet does act rashly sometimes such as when he kills Polonius. That seems out of character in some way, more like the way Laertes behaves, just do the deed and then worry about the results afterward. Hamlet is like Laertes as well in the focus on revenge, but Laertes says he would let nothing get in the way of his revenge whereas Hamlet lets anything and everything get in the way of his revenge. You almost wonder if Hamlet believes in his revenge, whereas Laertes seems to live for revenge—it's revenge or else. Laertes seems more ferocious and angry than Hamlet. He loves to yell great exaggerations. Like his speeches at the burial of Ophelia. But then Hamlet is like that too and wants to get into a contest with Laertes over who loved Ophelia more. They actually come to physical blows over the question and fight in her grave, which seems adolescent and foolish. Both of them can get out of control and hysterical. Both are hotheads. Two foolish young men who have so little control of their emotions that you know they're going to get into trouble. Hamlet himself seems to realize this when he tells his friend Horatio that he admires his calmness. It's not surprising that Hamlet and Laertes kill each other in the end. Maybe they're more alike than different when you stop to consider it. It's easy to think that Hamlet is the thinker and Laertes the man of rash action, but these differences hide many similarities.

After the student wrote this 10 minute piece on Hamlet and Laertes, he went back and edited the grammar, spelling, and punctuation to make the piece more readable, and a slightly edited version is printed here. Notice that nothing has been done to its organization. All of the thinking flows forward in a single paragraph, showing a lack of distinctions and lack of breaks in the thinking—exactly right for freewriting. The student began with the differences that divide Hamlet and Laertes and ended with their similarities. It surprised the student to learn that he had come up with so many similarities in the two characters, since he began the freewriting session convinced that Hamlet and Laertes are like night and day, a pair of opposites. Thus the freewriting fulfilled for this student the goal of exploration. Like any exploration, freewriting can produce surprises. Its value lies in part in its ability to plumb the depths of the mind where the unexpected dwells.

Freewriting on Literature Requires Depth of Knowledge

A caution is in order in this regard. Any of the brainstorming techniques such as freewriting work only if your mind is well stocked with knowledge of the literary work. If there is nothing but a few commonplaces about Hamlet in the depths of your mind, no amount of stirring the depths will come up with brilliant insights and original perceptions. Many of the brainstorming techniques were developed to help writers probe their own lives in writing personal and autobiographical material. Brainstorming works well for such enterprises because the materials are all found within the writer. They are his or her personal experiences, awaiting discovery. The same does not hold true of Hamlet's or Lady Macbeth's experiences, which do not come to us by intuition. You must first saturate yourself in Shakespeare's writing. Only then can you expect that freewriting will tap into a flow of knowledgeable discourse.

CLUSTERING

Clustering is another brainstorming technique for generating ideas and seeing relationships among ideas. You begin by writing in the center of a piece of paper the name of a character, a key word, an idea, or a brief quotation to be explored. Whatever you write down will be effective only if it creates a vivid image in your mind. The image then becomes central in your mind, as the words evoking it are in the center of the page. From that center you draw lines out to words, phrases, ideas, and other images that are associated with it in your mind. The more knowledgeable you are about the work of literature the more associations you will discover.

Clustering is sometimes called mapping, for it shows the roads of the mind as it branches out toward associations. On the page it has a spiderweb quality, pointing to the web-like connections of our mental life. Clustering pages will differ for each writer and for each effort. Keeping in mind that all such efforts vary greatly, look at the following as an example of how one student used the technique to explore associations surrounding Mr. Kurtz's words, "The horror! The horror!" in Joseph Conrad's *The Heart of Darkness*.

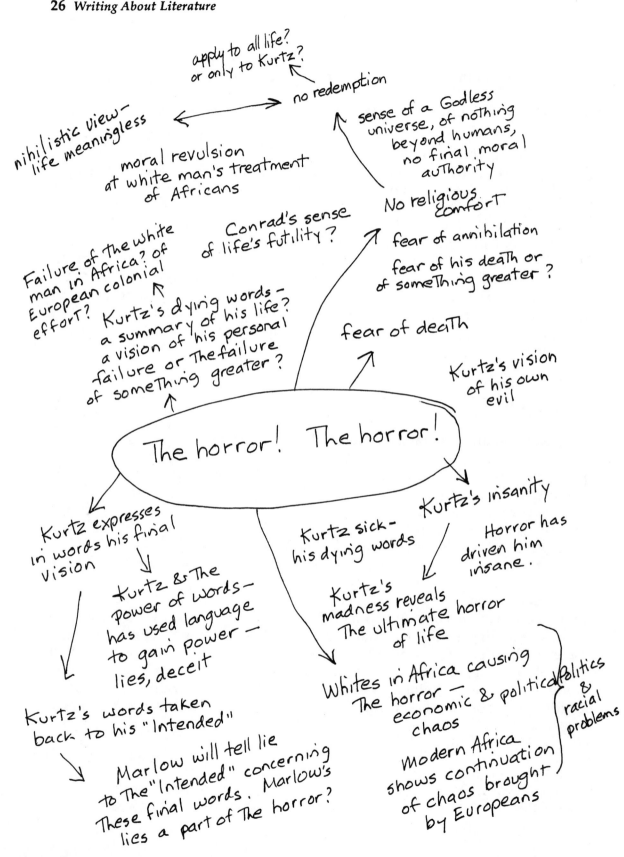

apply to all life?
or only to Kurtz?

no redemption

sense of a Godless universe, of nothing beyond humans, no final moral authority

nihilistic view – life meaningless

moral revulsion at white man's treatment of Africans

No religious comfort

fear of annihilation

fear of his death or of something greater?

Failure of the white man in Africa? of European colonial effort?

Conrad's sense of life's futility?

Kurtz's dying words – a summary of his life? a vision of his personal failure or the failure of something greater?

fear of death

Kurtz's vision of his own evil

The horror! The horror!

Kurtz expresses in words his final vision

Kurtz & the Power of words – has used language to gain power – lies, deceit

Kurtz sick – his dying words

Kurtz's insanity

Horror has driven him insane.

Kurtz's madness reveals the ultimate horror of life

Kurtz's words taken back to his "Intended"

Marlow will tell lie to the "Intended" concerning these final words. Marlow's lies a part of the horror?

Whites in Africa causing the horror – economic & political chaos

Politics & racial problems

Modern Africa shows continuation of chaos brought by Europeans

SECONDARY SOURCES

Secondary sources can be helpful in generating ideas for your papers in a number of ways. The most obvious of these ways—providing you directly with insights and understanding you did not arrive at on you own—is the least valuable for you as a student because it does your work for you. It also borders dangerously on plagiarism. If you borrow ideas and insights from a secondary source, you must credit your borrowing, even if you do not use the words of your source.

A more valuable way of using a secondary source is to find in it inspiration for your own thinking. The secondary source becomes a starting place for your own explorations. It points the way or provides a perspective. Consider, for example, the way the following student of Mark Twain's *The Adventures of Huckleberry Finn* found a direction in an article by Lionel Trilling (it is conveniently included as one of the essays in the *Norton Critical Edition* of the novel) on the significance of the river.

"Huck himself is the servant of the river-god, and he comes very close to being aware of the divine nature of the being he serves," is one quotation the student copied down from Trilling. He added, "The river itself is only divine . . . its nature seems to foster the goodness of those who love it and try to fit themselves to its ways. . . . To Huck much of the charm of the river life is human: it is the raft and the wigwam and Jim."

Reading this essay and applying its comments to his own understanding of the novel, the student came up with the following thesis: that the raft on which Huck and Jim travel down the Mississippi provides a place where Huck and Jim can live close to nature, at peace and in freedom. His paper was not a reworking of Trilling's essay, but used some of the critic's ideas as points of departure.

STUDENT PAPER

The Significance of the Raft in
The Adventures of Huckleberry Finn

In writing about *The Adventures of Huckleberry Finn*, Lionel Trilling has pointed out that the Mississippi River functions like a god, "a power which seems to have a mind and will of its own, and which . . appears to embody a great moral idea" ("The Greatness of Huckleberry Finn," in *Norton Critical Edition*, 312). This idea of the river as a god is in keeping with the ideas of several American writers of the 19th century, who saw in nature something divine. According to this view, the natural world, whether it is Thoreau's Walden Pond or Mark Twain's Mississippi, exerts a powerful formative influence on humans, a force that is moral and uplifting. Compared with the beneficial moral force of nature, society is often corrupting and limiting.

Even more important than the river as a source of great moral ideas is the raft on which Huck and Jim float down the Mississippi. It is on this raft that Huck comes to change his ideas about Jim and decides to risk the condemnation of his society and the possibility that he will go to hell in order to help free Jim. The raft and the river on which it floats provide an alternative way of seeing life from the moral codes of the towns along the shore, with their slavery and barbaric treatment of blacks. It is only by escaping from these shore towns and living alone with Jim on the raft that Huck can liberate himself from society's codes. As Trilling points out in the essay quoted above, aboard the raft "the boy and the Negro slave form a family, a primitive community—and it is a community of saints" (313).

Living on a raft that floats on the river, Huck and Jim find that there are no rules, no institutions, no artificial barriers. Morality on the river, instead of being based on tradition or the conventions of an artificial society, is based on feelings. If it feels right, then it is right. This is illustrated at the start of their journey when, feeling bad about stealing food, they resolve not to steal so much and Huck says, "We warn't feeling just right, before that, but it was all comfortable now" (112). Thus, because Jim and Huck do what their hearts tell them to do, life on the river is true and pure. But this reliance on feelings and intuition works only on the river while under the beneficial moral influence of this great moral force or god.

The chief moral benefit of life on the raft comes from the freedom and equality that the raft provides. The social distinctions of the shore towns and the division of human beings into free and slave disappear. Jim has freedom on the raft. As Huck puts it, life is "mighty free and easy and comfortable" (114) on a raft. And yet while he is experiencing freedom on the raft, Jim drifts right past freedom in society when they pass Cairo. This is an important point, for it shows that Jim is free only on the raft; he has floated beyond the chance for freedom in the world of the shore towns. It is as if Mark Twain were coming to realize in writing this novel that true freedom for these two characters could come only from the moral influence of nature embodied in the flowing river.

The moral influence of the river is unfortunately interrupted when the King and the Duke come aboard, because they bring with them the morality of the shore with its emphasis on money and greed and its distinctions of slave and freeman. The presence of these two men with their corrupt moral values shows that the little utopia of Huck and Jim, free and at peace on the river, is not permanent. The river flows on, as life does, and it leads to the world of immorality and slavery. Nevertheless, the beauty and freedom of Huck and Jim's life aboard the raft remains a lasting impression of the native goodness of nature and of their own native goodness. The moral force of the river is a natural fact, even though life in the shore towns ignores it.

The importance of this student paper's use of a secondary source lies in the impetus that Trilling's ideas gave to the student to come up with his own ideas. The student's paper is not a slavish imitation of Trilling's essay, but an original reworking of the critic's ideas plus the application of them to the student's own perceptions.

Disagreement with a Secondary Source

This essay shows a student using a secondary source to pursue a similar direction; however, students may be aroused to dispute a secondary source. Secondary sources can stimulate us to come up with our own ideas in opposition to a thesis we find limited or faulty. Many students, in fact, become most intensely involved in their writing when they can argue a point and attempt to refute the ideas of others. For example, a student who read in a secondary source that in many ways Huck Finn fails to free himself from the attitudes of his society and remains a racist at the end of Mark Twain's novel saw Huck in radically different terms. For him, Huck is a rebel and social critic, and the student set out to write a paper defending his vision and refuting the author of the essay. The first draft of his paper illustrates both the creative value of opposing views and the temptation to simplify ideas when in the grips of an argument.

"Mark Twain's Huck: Rebel and Social Critic" wrote the student as the title for his argumentative paper. Seeing Huck through the lens of adolescent rebellion, the student summarized his central argument: "Huck sees through the hypocrisy, racism, and stupidity of the adult world he finds on the shore. His raft becomes a little utopia from which he can criticize the society he finds when he steps foot on land."

This student's argument is appealing, because it makes a hero of a lovable character, but it embodies partial truths. It is simplistic, reducing Huck to a set of labels such as *rebel* and *honest* and adults to another set of labels—*hypocrites, racists, fools.* It ignores some facts of the novel—that the runaway slave, Jim, is an adult, but neither a hypocrite, a racist, nor a fool; that Huck himself utters racist statements; that the labels *rebel* and *social critic* do not fit Huck especially well because he does not in fact challenge or criticize the basic principles on which his society operates. The thesis of the paper overlooks the richness and complexity of the novel.

Nevertheless, the student's thesis about Huck as a rebel grows from something valuable and does capture an aspect of the novel. If the student turns his argument into a question—"In what ways does Huck rebel against his society and criticize its values?"—he can use it to open up worthwhile discussion of the novel. The student's argumentative flair, in other words, has produced a valuable perspective from his opposition to a secondary source.

In a second draft, the student revised his argument to show that while Huck performs many actions that show up the faults of the racist adult society, he is not a full-fledged rebel or social critic. Instead, Huck is an outsider. With this new thesis, the student was able to take a new intellectual position, one different from his original extreme perspective but still at odds with the secondary source that had originally aroused him to dispute. In this way the secondary source plus the student's willingness to revise his own ideas produced the ideas for the final paper.

3

AUDIENCE & PURPOSE

- • Defining Your Audience
- • Audience & Purpose
- • Your Teacher as Audience
- • Your Classmates as Audience

DEFINING YOUR AUDIENCE

Using Questions to Define Audience & Purpose

The author of an effective literary paper should have in mind the following questions:

1. Who is the audience for this writing?
2. What standards will my audience use to judge my writing?
3. What do I want to tell my audience?
4. What is the purpose of this writing?
5. How can I express my purpose to my audience?

These questions, starting with audience and ending with the thesis (what you want to say about a topic) and issues of organization and style (how to express yourself) are closely interrelated. Often student writers do not stop to ask themselves these questions about audience and purpose. They assume that the audience and purpose are supplied by the assignment. The audience? The teacher, of course. The purpose? To fulfill an assignment (e.g., to answer the assigned question about the relationship of Huck and Jim in Mark Twain's *The Adventures of Huckleberry Finn* or to discuss the view of nature expressed in Emily Dickinson's poem, "I Taste a Liquor Never Brewed").

Even when the audience and the purpose of the writing have been to a certain extent dictated by the nature of the academic exercise, such questions are worth your attention as a student writer. Consider, for example, the differences you feel as you write the following:

1. a page of personal reflections in your journal;
2. a letter to a friend your own age;
3. an essay used as part of your college application;
4. an article for your school newspaper;
5. a research paper in history.

Many of the differences you feel as you write in these different ways arise because of your sense of the audience. Even if you have not reflected on these differences in audience and have not put into words your understanding of who will read your writing, you undoubtedly have an operational sense of who your audience is. As you write in your journal you feel the intimacy and relaxation that comes from writing for yourself. By contrast, writing an essay for college admissions may make you tense and self-conscious, fearful of a nit-picking and highly critical audience with enormous power over your future. Your attitude toward your audience is related to your purpose; equally obvious is that the audience and your attitude influence your word choices. Your writer's instincts tell you that the slang you might use in a letter to a friend is inappropriate in the essay for college and in the history paper.

AUDIENCE & PURPOSE

Becoming Conscious of Your Reading Audience

The question of audience carries important consequences. It is difficult to decide how you will proceed and what points you will make without knowing who will be reading your material. Whether you are conscious of your audience or not, your audience helps to determine your purpose. Thus you help to sharpen your sense of purpose by bringing into sharper focus your understanding of who will be reading your material. Questions such as whether or not your writing will develop an argument or thesis, what argumentative approach to take, and how you will word it, depend in large part on your sense of who will be reading your words.

The Writer as Audience: Journal Writing

Journal writing often has only the author as an audience. As a consequence, journal writing is usually less formal than other kinds of writing on literature. It may lack the sense of purpose that comes from organizing your ideas into arguments to support a thesis. Good journal writing is often exploratory, an act of discovery rather than of argument. The author sets out like an explorer in undiscovered country to enjoy the views, not to reach a known destination or to plant a flag on the highest peak. Even if you write journal entries that will be shared with your classmates and teacher, you typically use an informal style and proceed as if you the writer were the primary audience. The sense of the audience reading over your shoulder need not be developed in journal writing. In fact, much of the charm of journal writing comes from the lack of self-consciousness that results from ignoring the audience.

Much journal writing can be seen as self-expression. Although writing that is designed basically as self-expression may also communicate with others, its primary purpose is not communication. Drawing distinctions between writing as self-expression and writing as communication can help sharpen your sense of how an audience influences your writing.

Editing Your Prewriting to Communicate with an Audience

Most of your prewriting exercises share with journal writing the sense of exploring a topic for your eyes only. When you begin to reflect on your prewriting exercises and draw on them to draft your paper, however, you will need to introduce the concept of an audience. As you ask yourself who will be reading your material, you will also consider how you will communicate with your readers—how you will organize and phrase your writing so your ideas are clear and your arguments convincing.

Questions about how you will phrase your writing pertain to the complex topic of style, which is covered in Chapter 9. Your sense of your audience has a major impact on your style. To assess that impact, consider how differently you speak when you address the following people: (1) yourself, (2) your close friends, (3) your parents, and (4) your teachers.

YOUR TEACHER AS AUDIENCE

Your Teacher's Expression of Expectations & Standards

Your teacher often helps you understand his or her role as audience by spelling out expectations. Consider, for example, the teacher who has given students the following assignment:

> • "Write eight to ten pages of clear prose supporting or disagreeing with the idea that Hamlet is mad during much of the action of the play. Be sure to refer to specific scenes and actions to support your argument, and use quotations generously. Type or print your paper. It will be judged by its grammar, word choices, logic, and understanding of the literature. Revise and proofread your paper carefully. Careless mistakes such as spelling errors will weaken your grade."

The teacher who drew up this assignment has gone to some lengths to spell out his role as audience. If you were writing a paper to meet the demands of this assignment, you might feel daunted by the rigor and explicitness of the assignment and the demand for careful writing, but at least you would know your reader's standards and what you must do to please him.

Learning to Know Your Teacher as Audience

Teachers do not form an anonymous audience. Novelists and poets and journalists often have only a general idea of their readers, but students writing for a specific teacher can put a face and a name to their primary audience, which is at once both an advantage and a drawback. It is an advantage because it gives you advance warning of the standards by which you will be judged; it is a disadvantage because you may be intimidated by your teacher.

Whatever your feelings, you will improve your chances of success in writing if you take steps to know your audience as well as possible, which in the case of academic writing means knowing your teacher's expectations and standards. What writing of yours or of a classmate has this teacher admired? Why? What writing has he or she given a low grade? What critical comments did the teacher offer to explain the grade and to point out problems and weaknesses? Many teachers spend time on these comments, and they go some distance to express their expectations. They are written to point out generally accepted writing standards, such as the importance in formal writing of avoiding run-on sentences and fragments. Thus knowing your teacher as your audience means in part knowing the formal rules of grammar and composition. Because your teacher's standards are not primarily personal in the sense of being peculiar to him or her, the problem of the capricious reading public with which would-be best-selling novelists or journalists must deal is largely absent from academic writing.

Your Teacher as the Expression of General Standards

This recognition that your teacher's expectations and standards grow from something general can provide you with a clearer sense of what is expected of you, because the standards by which you will be read and evaluated are those that inform English courses and textbooks. They are shared standards. Thus to know one English teacher's standards well is to know the standards of English teachers generally. Of course there are individual differences. For example, some teachers object to the use of the first person in formal essays, while others accept it. Knowing your teacher as audience means to a certain extent knowing such individual preferences. But such differences are usually small and primarily matters of emphasis. Most of the standards your teacher uses to judge your papers are shared by everyone in the profession.

Gaining Responses from Your Teacher

To understand your teacher's standards more thoroughly, ask your teacher for a conference on your paper as you work on it. Most teachers welcome such requests. Show your teacher your thesis, your outline, and your rough draft and ask for his or her responses. These responses can help to sharpen your sense of what is expected of you. Many teachers ask for your written work in stages. As you receive back the various stages, read your teacher's comments closely. Not only will this develop your understanding of your teacher as a reader of your papers, but it will also help you to grasp more thoroughly the generally accepted standards for good writing that your teacher upholds, and it can contribute to your sense that good writing is often a collaborative effort.

YOUR CLASSMATES AS AUDIENCE

Sharing Your Papers with Your Classmates

In many English classes students share their papers with their classmates. Perhaps they read them aloud in class, or they may exchange papers during a peer editing session. Sometimes student papers are photocopied and distributed to everyone in the class. Enlarging the audience to include students has benefits for student writers because it allows them to write for a more general audience, for contemporaries as well as for teachers. In this sense, your classmates become colleagues, a word that helps to focus them as readers who share your struggles and know the ordeal you encountered as you worked on your paper.

Your Classmates as Colleagues

You can often improve your writing by developing a sense of collegiality with your classmates. It is an attitude encouraged by seeing that your classmates are working with you in the education taking place in your school, that you are sharing your understanding and your words with a sympathetic audience while you are working on developing your abilities. It is important to realize that the concept of a colleague, unlike that of a friend, implies standards. Where a friend may remain silent, a colleague may voice criticism of your writing. Indeed, a colleague *should* offer criticism if he or she recognizes that your writing is vague, incorrect, weak, or limited. A colleague wants you to improve. Where a friend might say inwardly, "I don't want to point out any of the weaknesses in this writing, because the author is my friend, and I don't want to jeopardize our friendship," a colleague takes a different approach. Colleagues see one another professionally, and they are as committed to upholding the standards of the profession (in this case, the standards of good writing) as they are to maintaining the friendships among colleagues. If they are to act as your colleagues, your classmates will need to see that they do not "help" you by telling you that weak or flawed writing is fine as it is and needs no revision.

Considering Your Teacher as a Colleague

Ideally a student might consider the teacher to be part of an audience of colleagues. Then the teacher can be seen as a student (which is the truth of the matter) and recognized as someone struggling with the process of learning. Then, too, the teacher's comments and judgments can be viewed as part of the teacher's interest in sharing the student's struggles to come up with valuable ideas and find the words to express them. The teacher as colleague provides a model of how we benefit from measuring our work by professional standards that are shared by all of us, not imposed in arbitrary fashion by those in authority over the young.

4

DEVELOPING A THESIS

- • **Why Build a Paper Around a Thesis?**
- • **Finding a Topic Suitable for a Thesis**
- • **Plot Summary & Thesis**
- • **The Thesis as Assertion**
- • **Revising the Thesis as You Write**
- • **Supporting the Thesis**

WHY BUILD A PAPER AROUND A THESIS?

A good literary paper has a main point or central idea. Although not all literary papers need the argumentative thrust associated with the defense of a thesis, all do benefit from a clear point of view. Lacking a point of view, a paper wanders. You may find as the writer that when you lack a thesis or a clear purpose you struggle along with no direction. If you feel this as you write, you can be sure that your readers will feel it as they read.

Most of your teachers who ask for formal literary essays will expect you to organize your thinking around a thesis. Look on a thesis as in part an organizing principle and in part an aspect of the intellectual content of your paper. A thesis gives a paper intellectual vigor. It carries you along as you write and your readers along as they try to follow your argument. It is like a compass; by consulting it frequently, it reminds you of where you are going and keeps you on course.

FINDING A TOPIC SUITABLE FOR A THESIS

Beginning with Your Interests

Before creating a thesis statement you must find a topic for your paper. Finding a topic means of course finding something that interests you. Begin all of your writing with your own interests. If you have limited interest in your topic, then you will bring limited energies to the paper, and it will seem flat and boring, both to you and to your readers. Thus your first task is to come up with interesting ideas—the processes of Chapters 1 and 2. Once you come up with ideas about the work of literature, focus on one or two that awaken the most energy in you. Even if you find the work of literature generally flat and dull, there may be some corner of it that draws your interest: possibly a minor character, or some aspect of the setting, or the way certain images recur.

Working with an Assigned Topic

If you have been assigned a topic, then you still need to find the aspects of the topic that most arouse you. In addition, you will want to refine and limit the topic so that it is of manageable length and so that you can create from it a focused thesis. A topic that is vague and unwieldy cannot provide you with a clear thesis.

Brainstorming for a Main Topic

Let's assume you have been asked to come up with a topic on *Antigone* by Sophocles. You begin with your interest in the title character, who strikes you as passionate in an admirable way. You know that you like her as a character, but you are not entirely sure why. You begin, in other words, with little more than an undefined response, a feeling, an attraction to a character, which is where many writers begin. How do you move from such a vague and sketchy beginning to something as pointed as a thesis?

Following some of the brainstorming techniques of Chapter 2, you might write the name Antigone on a sheet of paper or on the computer screen and write a series of questions about the character, such as the following:

STUDENT BRAINSTORMING

Sophocles' Antigone

What motivates Antigone?
What makes her so headstrong?
What does she want to prove?
How does she differ from her sister?

How could two such different women be sisters?
Why is she so abrupt and rude to her sister?
What exactly are her religious beliefs?
Why does she care so much about her dead brother?
What are the sacred laws she speaks of?
What is the significance for her of the realm of the dead?

Your list of questions could be much longer, but this list is long enough to suggest the kinds of questions that can supply you with choices sufficiently limited to allow you to write with a clear direction.

Let us say that the questions that most attract you from the above list are those that bring Antigone into contrast with her sister, Ismene. To sharpen this contrast, you write both names on a sheet of paper or on the computer screen and dig out of the text those quotations from the two sisters' speeches that express their characters. The names and the quotations then become the inspiration for further brainstorming that can help sharpen your thinking into a thesis. Here, for example, are the results of one student's brainstorming on the comparison of Antigone and Ismene:

STUDENT BRAINSTORMING

Antigone

"Creon is not strong enough to stand in my way."

passion and courage
feels her own strength—willing to challenge the king
certain of her convictions
powerful religious sense that gives her self-confidence
scornful of authority and those who oppose her
quick to take action

Ismene

"We are only women,
We cannot fight with men . . .
We must give in to the law . . .
I am helpless: I must yield
to those in authority."

weak and passive
helplessness, uncertainty
refuses to challenge authority
slow to act
law-abiding, a good(?) and peaceful citizen

Turning a Topic into a Thesis

Looking over the results of her brainstorming, the student decided she would write on the topic of Antigone's religious convictions compared with Ismene's lack of religious convictions. This is still a topic, not a thesis. It is, however, on the threshold of a thesis; it is focused and limited in scope. The student found it an easy matter to state the topic so that it became the following thesis:

Antigone's religious convictions give her the courage to defy secular authority and contrast with Ismene's lack of religious convictions, which makes her weak and yielding.

Sharpening the Thesis

The student was required to submit this thesis to her teacher before proceeding with her paper. Her teacher suggested that the thesis might be improved by further limitation. Perhaps she needed only the first half of her statement as her thesis. She could bring in the comparisons with Ismene in the body of the paper, but by focusing on Antigone only she might find she had a more focused paper. As a result, the student's final thesis was this more limited statement:

Antigone's religious convictions give her the courage to defy Creon and secular authority.

PLOT SUMMARY & THESIS

Avoiding Plot Summary

A common difficulty in writing papers about stories, novels, and plays arises when students offer plot summary rather than a thesis. Plot summary is rarely called for in a critical paper. The faulty use of plot summary especially tempts the student who sets out to write about a play or novel without a thesis. If you have no clear argument to offer, then you can easily slip into this summarizing for lack of anything better to say. For example: "After Huck escapes from Pap, he travels down the Mississippi on a raft. He is joined by Jim, the runaway slave, and the two of them have a series of adventures. Many times Huck must do some fast talking to save Jim. Then the King and the Duke come aboard the raft. . . ." Such plot summary suggests a lack of perspective and an absence of critical inquiry.

There follows a sample first paragraph in a student paper that lacks a sharply defined thesis and as a consequence slips into plot summary. The title of the paper, "The character of Sophocles' Antigone," also states what the student believed was the thesis of the paper. However, the title is the topic, not a thesis, and although the first sentence offers what could be considered a thesis, at best it is only a general thesis, one that needs sharpening to give focus to the writer as he proceeds with his paper.

STUDENT PARAGRAPH

The Character of Sophocles' Antigone

Antigone is a strong character who does what she thinks is right. When she learns that Creon has proclaimed a law prohibiting the burial of her brother, Polyneices, she does not agree with this and decides she will bury him. She does this by herself since her sister, Ismene, will not help her. She goes out onto the battlefield and puts dust over her brother's body. When she is caught doing this she is brought before Creon, where she admits performing the action and refuses to confess that it was wrong. So Creon puts her to death. She goes to her death as a martyr, proud of her act of reverence for her brother.

Turning Plot Summary into a Thesis

The above material on Antigone amounts largely to a summary of Antigone's actions. Notice the way it follows the chronology of the play, moving from one action to the next as the play moves. It is acceptable summary, but it lacks a point. It wanders from whatever thesis it might be attempting to advance and gives the impression that in fact there is no thesis. The statement, "Antigone is a strong character who does what she thinks is right," is too general to provide much direction for the student. Its use of the adjective *strong* to describe Antigone adds little information and leaves the reader wondering, "Strong in what way?"

When the student was asked to define further his view of Antigone as a "strong character," he stated that Antigone's strength was seen in her defiant courage. She showed her strength when she refused to follow Creon's orders. Working with this idea of her courage, he came up with a thesis to rewrite his paper:

Antigone's courage makes her willing to defy Creon and accept the punishment of death.

This clarified and more focused thesis gave the student something to build on, and in the revision the student improved the paper considerably. The revision of the paragraph reads as follows:

REVISED STUDENT PARAGRAPH

Antigone's Courage

Antigone is a strong, courageous character who does what she believes is morally right. She needs great courage to perform the actions she believes are right, because her view of what is right is directly in conflict with Creon, the king of Thebes. Creon has proclaimed that anyone who buries Antigone's brother, Polyneices, will be put to death. Believing this to be an immoral proclamation, Antigone has the courage to go out and bury Polyneices and to risk her own death for what she believes in. The force of her courage is great enough so that she is willing to do this alone. She asks her sister, Ismene, to join her in this action, but Ismene refuses and advises Antigone against performing the burial. Antigone refuses to listen to her, showing how brave and determined she is.

Notice that by focusing on a thesis the student has enlarged on the significance of Antigone's actions rather than just summarizing them. As a consequence he wrote more on Antigone's act of burying her brother and saved for a later paragraph the courage she showed in admitting the crime and accepting its consequences. Although there are still weaknesses in the paragraph (it includes no direct quotations, its wording is repetitive, and it stumbles into a wording problem when it compares Antigone's "view of what is right" with Creon, rather than with Creon's view), it now shows that the student has thought about the significance of the actions he describes. He has something to say, and his paragraph makes a point.

THE THESIS AS ASSERTION

Stating the Thesis as an Assertion

The thesis concerning Antigone is stated in a complete sentence. A topic becomes a thesis by taking the form of an assertion that can be written as a sentence.

Comparing a Topic with a Thesis

In contrast to a thesis, a topic can be put in a word (Antigone, Ophelia, Pip), in a few words (Antigone's courage, Ophelia's death, Pip's great expectations), or in a phrase (Antigone's opposition to Ismene, Ophelia's escape through suicide, Pip's expectations of life in London). Topics often work their way into the title of a paper, whereas a thesis is typically stated in the introductory paragraph or early in the body of the essay.

Some possible theses created from the above topics might be stated as follows:

1. Antigone's courage contrasts with Ismene's fearfulness.
2. Ophelia's weakness of character is shown in her escape through suicide.
3. Pip's great expectations of his life in London cut him off from his true friends, Joe and Biddy.

TOPIC AND THESES FOR A PAPER ON *ROMEO AND JULIET*

Here is a topic for a paper on Shakespeare's *Romeo and Juliet* plus theses that have been created from the topic:

Topic
The role of the adults in Shakespeare's *Romeo and Juliet*

General Thesis
Adults mislead the young lovers in Shakespeare's *Romeo and Juliet*.

Limited Theses
1. The nurse and Friar Laurence mislead the young lovers in Shakespeare's *Romeo and Juliet*.
2. The nurse gives poor advice to Juliet in Shakespeare's *Romeo and Juliet*.
3. Friar Laurence misleads the young lovers in Shakespeare's *Romeo and Juliet*.
4. Through his hot temper and impetuous actions, Juliet's father becomes a major cause of the suffering and death of his daughter in Shakespeare's *Romeo and Juliet*.

Notice that the first thesis on Romeo and Juliet (that adults mislead the young lovers) casts a wide net. To be faithful to its full implications you would need to discuss not just the nurse and Friar Laurence but also Romeo and Juliet's parents and the prince, whose influence is different from that of the other adults in the play. Thus you would need to blunt the sharp point of the thesis. You would find that to be honest to the play, you would need to introduce various qualifications, and you would have your hands full dealing with all of the ways in which the adults mislead the young lovers. At the very least you would find that there is more material to cover with such a broad thesis than you would have time for in the usual literary paper.

Read this as a warning against a general thesis. Look on a general thesis as a first step in refining and limiting what you want to cover.

The more limited theses on *Romeo and Juliet* would allow you to narrow your focus and explore the topic in depth. You might worry that the more limited theses would be too narrow to produce a full paper—a common worry among inexperienced writers, who often think that in order to come up with the required number of words they need a broad topic and a general thesis. But a broad topic and a general thesis invite vagueness. You want to write in depth and detail, not with sweeping generalizations, and you will be helped by a thesis that sharply limits its scope, points clearly to one or two characters, and focuses on two or three scenes rather than the entire action of the play.

Experienced writers would recognize that the last thesis concerning Juliet's father's "hot temper and impetuous actions" would generate the most sharply focused paper. It would lead the writer at once to certain scenes and to the quotations that would support it. It would provide the fewest complications and be the easiest to organize and support.

REVISING THE THESIS AS YOU WRITE

You may begin work with one thesis and then discover through your preliminary writing and better understanding of the material that your thesis is too large and vague or that you no longer agree with it. Or you may find through your writing another idea more valuable and interesting. In such cases, come up with a new thesis and write a new draft. Writing is a way of focusing and clarifying your thinking, and it is only natural that your thinking and your thesis will change as you work on a topic.

Limiting the Thesis to a Single Sentence

If your thesis grows to two or more sentences you may have something too broad and complicated on your hands. A thesis that resists encapsulating in a single sentence will likely prove too ambitious for a short paper. Or it may lack clear focus. Keep working to refine it until it can be stated in a forceful sentence.

Revising the Thesis at the End of the First Draft

When you have finished your first draft, reread it to see if it does in fact develop and support the thesis as you intended. If not, what happened? Did you wander away from your thesis in your writing? Or did the thesis statement turn out to be the wrong one? At the end of your first draft, try rewording your thesis in a fresh way to capture the argument that you developed in the draft. If your newly worded thesis differs from your original statement, then you need to reassess your thesis or else reexamine the logic of your argument.

Stating the Thesis in the Opening Paragraph

Once you have stated your thesis clearly, move directly into your topic by building your opening paragraph around the thesis statement. Although there are other ways to use a thesis—it may be introduced at the end or in the middle of an essay—it usually helps you and your reader if you state your thesis early. Consider the way the following paragraph lets the reader know at once where it is going through the clear and succinct statement of its thesis:

STUDENT PARAGRAPH

Oedipus in Sophocles' *Oedipus Rex* is a great man because of his moral courage in accepting the consequences of his actions. Although he has committed terrible crimes and must be considered a criminal, his courageous drive to know the truth about himself and to accept the consequences of his previous actions elevate him to the level of tragic greatness. Like any tragic hero he has flaws in his character, but these do not cancel out his admirable qualities or reduce his stature.

Here the student has stated the thesis clearly and offered it in the opening sentence. Although it is not necessary for the thesis to be stated in the first sentence or even in the first paragraph, building it into your paper early in the writing helps you in many ways. Contrast the paragraph above with the following, which lacks a thesis:

STUDENT PARAGRAPH

Oedipus Rex, written by Sophocles, was based on the journeys and quests of the main character, Oedipus. Throughout the play, Oedipus, King of Thebes, displayed impatience and irrationality when in conflict with certain people, namely Iocaste and Teiresias. One would think that Oedipus was selfish, since he was always demanding to know things immediately. However, he was merely impatient, and his lack of tolerance proved his downfall.

This opening paragraph gives the reader little help in suggesting what is to come in the body of the paper. Is this student planning to discuss the journeys and quests of Oedipus? His irrationality? His selfishness? His lack of tolerance? Lacking a central thesis, the paragraph tosses out several ideas but focuses on none of them, and it leaves the impression that the author is not certain what he wants to say.

SUPPORTING THE THESIS

Turning to the Evidence in the Text

Once you have stated your thesis in a sentence and perhaps written an introductory paragraph showing how you mean to apply the thesis and argue its defense, turn to the text to find evidence for it. View your thesis as a statement to be argued and recognize that all argument rests on evidence. Without evidence an argument falls; it is exposed as mere assertion of opinion. The primary evidence for a thesis on a work of literature must arise from the literature itself. The evidence must be clear and specific: references to the literary work that cite characters, scenes, actions, and gestures, and frequent quotations that anchor the argument to the text.

For example, the first student quoted above supported the thesis in the opening paragraph by quoting directly from the play in the second paragraph. The first and second paragraphs follow:

STUDENT PARAGRAPHS

Oedipus in Sophocles' *Oedipus Rex* is a great man because of his moral courage in accepting the consequences of his actions. Although he has committed terrible crimes and must be considered a criminal, his courageous drive to know the truth about himself and to accept the consequences of his previous actions elevate him to the level of tragic greatness. Like any tragic hero he has flaws in his character, but these do not cancel out his admirable qualities or reduce his stature.

Scene III brings into clear focus the driving force of Oedipus as he searches for the murderer of Laios and the clues to the mystery of his own identity. Iocaste, his wife and mother, tries to prevent him from learning these things, for she has recognized their terrible truth, but Oedipus insists that "the truth must be made known." When Iocaste points out that "everything I say is for your own good," Oedipus responds, "My own good snaps my patience, then; I want none of it," showing his willingness to suffer in order to gain the truth. Soon he, like Iocaste, recognizes that she is his mother, but he does not shrink from accepting this terrible recognition. Where most people would offer evasions, or defensive arguments, or try to cover up the facts, Oedipus takes his punishment like a hero, accepting full responsibility for who he is and what he has done.

Support for the thesis includes references to Scene III and the actions and characters in the scene along with the direct quotations. The quotations, although brief, focus the reader's attention on the text and tie the author's commentary to the literature in a convincing way.

If you cannot find direct quotations for your thesis, or you cannot turn to specific scenes or episodes that demonstrate its validity, you probably have an unsupportable thesis, and you should look for a different one. Your thesis should be a direct outgrowth of the literary work, and at every step in arguing your case you should lead your readers back into the text. A major goal of literary criticism is to illuminate the literary text. If it does not lead the readers back to the original work with fresh insights, it has accomplished little. Thus after offering your readers the benefit of your conclusions or judgments, show in specific ways how these apply to the literary work.

Consider the way the following two paragraphs (the first two) in a paper on Nathaniel Hawthorne's Hester Prynne in *The Scarlet Letter* moves directly to the novel to demonstrate the thesis:

STUDENT PARAGRAPHS

Hester Prynne's Strengths

Hester Prynne may be seen by the Puritan community as a wicked, fallen woman and treated as an outcast, but her strength of character allows her to exert a strong moral influence on her community. The very circumstances under which she must live demand great strength and psychological resistance. She must endure the hatred of the people and public exposure and must wear a symbol that always reminds her of the hours of shame on the pillory. Yet from the start she rises above these circumstances and later forces the community to recognize her as an important part of the town. Nathaniel Hawthorne shows us Hester's great strength at the beginning when he says, "She repelled him by an action marked with natural dignity and force of character, and stepped into the open air, as if by her own free will" (24). Once on the pillory, she maintains herself calmly "supported by an unnatural tension of nerves, and by all the combative energy of her character, which enabled her to convert the scene into a kind of lurid triumph" (25). This "combative energy" that gives her strength to "convert the scene" into a "triumph" provides a key to her character; it is this same energy that allows her to convert her entire outcast, despised life into a kind of triumph.

This triumph and force of character are seen when Hester becomes such a superior seamstress that even the governor calls upon her skills. She contributes money to charity and takes food to the poor, even though "the bitter-hearted pauper threw back a gibe in requital of the food brought regularly to his door" (156). During any calamity, Hester comes forward, providing help. She stays at Governor Winthrop's bedside until he dies peacefully, showing how her influence reaches from the lowest to the highest levels of her community.

This paper supports its thesis about Hester's strength with two kinds of references to the novel: (1) direct quotations and (2) references to specific actions, such as the mention of her taking food to the poor and sitting at Governor Winthrop's bedside. These references accomplish three of the goals of a good critical paper: (1) They make the paper's thesis forceful, clear, and specific; (2) they draw the reader's mind back to the novel; and (3) they illuminate the text under discussion.

5

USING QUOTATIONS

- The Importance of Direct Quotations
- Frequency of Quotations
- Length of Quotations
- Setting Quotations into the Text
- Documenting Quotations
- Paraphrasing Instead of Quoting

THE IMPORTANCE OF DIRECT QUOTATIONS

Using Quotations at Each Step of Composing Your Paper

With each step you take in composing a paper on literature, you gain benefits by working closely with direct quotations from the text. Quotations provide a foundation for all writing about literature. In your first steps of close reading and note-taking, you lay the groundwork for your composition by pulling quotations from the text. As you prepare for class and take notes in class, you should underline passages from the author being studied and copy many of them into your notebook. Include quotations in your journal. Try opening your journal entry with a direct quotation that becomes the basis for your commentary. Brainstorming techniques often focus on a quotation. An excellent way to begin a draft on a computer includes the writing of a quotation at the top of the screen and allowing this to inspire the composition. If you find yourself stuck in coming up with a topic for a paper, then turn to a favorite quotation from the work you are to discuss and let the quotation help to suggest possible topics.

Creating a Computer File or Notebook of Quotations

If you are using a computer to write your paper, use a computer notepad or file to gather and store relevant quotations (see Chapter 1). Consider the following collections of quotations from Shakespeare's *Romeo and Juliet*. The student who gathered these quotations was writing a paper on the sense of doom that foreshadows the death of the two lovers. He wanted to demonstrate that the play indicates their deaths are destined by the heavens or the stars. He included the file of quotations in a computer folder entitled *Romeo and Juliet* that contained a second file for the draft of his paper. He found it easy to move from the paper to the file of quotations, copy the quotations, and paste them into his paper as he needed them. Notice that he has included with the quotations the act, scene, and line numbers within parentheses, the preferred way of documenting quotations. When he copied the quotations and pasted them into his paper, the documentation was automatically included. Compare this to the more laborious process of gathering quotations longhand in a notebook or on note cards and then copying them again in the paper.

COMPUTER FILE

Romeo and Juliet: Quotations

Thesis: The play indicates from the beginning that Romeo and Juliet are doomed by the stars or the heavens to a tragic ending.

> From forth the fatal loins of these two foes
> A pair of star-crossed lovers take their life. (Prologue, lines 5,6)

> Romeo: . . . my mind misgives
> Some consequence, yet hanging in the stars,
> Shall bitterly begin his fearful date
> With this night's revels and expire the term
> Of a despised life, closed in my breast,
> By some vile forfeit of untimely death. (1.4.106-111)

> Romeo: Then I defy you, stars! (5.1.24)

> Friar: A greater power than we can contradict
> Hath thwarted our intents. (5.3.153-154)

> Prince: Heaven finds means to kill your joys with love. (5.3.293)

This collection of quotations allowed the student to create a well supported paper that defended his thesis with the evidence of Shakespeare's words.

Notice that the quotations are brief—one or two lines—except for the six lines from Romeo, allowing the student to weave them into his text easily. The student used the longer quotation from Romeo as the basis for an entire paragraph. After the student assembled these quotations the paper moved smoothly. To organize his writing he needed only to move from one quotation to the next.

If you use a computer for a collection of quotations, print out the quotations on paper before writing your rough draft. You want to be able to see all of your quotations as you work on your draft.

Quotations as the Support for Your Thesis

By the time you have reached the first-draft stage, you should have a clear sense of what quotations you will be using to support your thesis. Consider direct quotations to be essential building blocks of your development. If you write a draft without the use of direct quotations, then you may wander from the text you are purportedly discussing, and you may later face difficulties trying to find quotations to support your conclusions. You may discover that in fact there are no quotations that really fit your conclusions, because your argument has moved away from the text.

When you begin with quotations as the foundation of your writing and gather them in abundance, digging out more than you think you will need in your final paper, you will find your quotations guiding your writing. Your paper will remain anchored to the text as you work, and you will have little trouble supporting your conclusions.

Notice how the following student discussion of Iocaste in Sophocles' *Oedipus Rex* offers some valuable conclusions but no evidence. Lacking direct quotations, the paragraph is vague and remote from the text.

STUDENT PARAGRAPH

Iocaste is too weak to stand up to the truth. She hears the truth but runs away from it. She is a coward, taking the easy way out. If she had the courage to stand up to the truth, she could have provided some comfort for Oedipus in his troubles. Instead she gave up on him. She gave him no help when he most needed it, which shows how weak she is.

This paragraph lacks references to specific actions as well as direct quotations. When does Iocaste hear the truth but run from it? In writing of "the easy way out," does the student mean Iocaste's suicide? The student could have avoided the uncertainties and vagueness of this paragraph by grounding it in the text, which she did in a revised version as follows:

REVISED STUDENT PARAGRAPH

Iocaste is too weak to stand up to the truth, as she shows when she attempts to stop the shepherd from telling what he knows about her husband's parentage. "Do not listen to this man!" she cries out to Oedipus in Scene III. "Let us have no more questioning!" When Oedipus insists on continuing the investigation, Iocaste turns away, escapes from the direct confrontation with the truth, and commits suicide. Her suicide shows that her courage has failed. If she had been able to stand up to the truth, she could have provided some comfort for Oedipus in his troubles. Instead she abandoned him.

By drawing the reader into a direct consideration of the action and language of the play, the student has greatly improved the original paragraph. The paragraph now has substance, not just assertion and opinion. Furthermore, in the revised paragraph the student has done more than just add two direct quotations and references to specific actions; she has developed the paragraph. Where the first version is sketchy and vague, the second strikes us as reasoned and thoughtful. This development consists of little more than direct quotation and specific references to the text, but so important are they to giving substance to the argument that they transform the paragraph.

FREQUENCY OF QUOTATION

Frequent References to the Text

How often should you quote directly from the text you are discussing? There is no hard-and-fast rule to follow here, aside from the general principle that you should quote the texts that you are discussing frequently. Quote whenever you offer a generalization, conclusion, or important insight. Referring to the text continuously helps you to orient your ideas. If you are discussing a play or novel, then your frequent direct references to the text help you and your reader to focus on the chronology and movement of the action. If you are discussing a poem, then quotation moves you and your reader into a direct contemplation of the language of the poet. Most students fail to quote often enough. Rarely do students quote too frequently.

Many of us feel more secure if we have a rule to follow, and in regard to the frequency of quoting the text, here is a general one: Quote the text once for every 100 of your own words. In a paper of 1,000 words, you should quote the text about 10 times. This does not mean 10 large chunks of quotation. At times a single quoted word is enough.

There is nothing magical or authoritative in such a rule of procedure, and in fact it is hardly a rule at all. Thus you may write a 1,000-word literary essay that needs only 5 direct quotes from your text, or only 3; you might write another paper of that length requiring 25 quotations.

LENGTH OF QUOTATIONS

Quoting One or Two Lines

How much of the text should you quote at one time? Sometimes a word or a line will do, and sometimes you need to include a generous sampling. For most occasions, one or two lines will provide all you need. Notice how in the following discussion of the poetry of Wordsworth the student documented her thesis with a single two-line quotation:

STUDENT PARAGRAPH

Wordsworth believes that humans are born in a state of grace, a blessed condition superior in many ways to adulthood. He sees the newborn child as close to God, the religious and vital source of universal life. Wordsworth thus looks back to birth as a sacred moment because of the closeness of the newborn to the "glory" of the universe. He writes, "Not in utter nakedness, / But trailing clouds of glory do we come." The infant is closer to this heavenly source of life than is the child, and the child is closer than the adult. Thus in Wordsworth's view, growing up is a movement away from this "glory," away from God.

The student ties her own preceding discussion to the quoted lines by using the word "glory," then repeats this word in the discussion following. The paragraph with its quoted lines is a good example of how to use a brief quotation as the core of your own discussion, a nucleus around which you create your analysis.

Using Longer Quotations

When you discuss the style of a writer, you may need to quote longer pieces to give your readers a taste of the style. Or, when you want to show the conflict between two characters in a work of fiction or drama, you may need a generous sampling of dialogue. Longer quotations from the text help if you are examining an author's philosophy or some subtle steps in the author's logic.

For a sample of a longer quotation, here is a student writing on Thomas Hardy's tragic vision in *Tess of the d'Urbervilles*:

STUDENT PARAGRAPHS

Hardy sees life as tragedy. Pain and disappointment beset his characters. Coincidence works against them. His characters suffer at the hands of biological and social forces beyond their control. A cruel fate sits and mocks their efforts. They suffer especially if they're sensitive, like Tess. Everywhere in his novel Hardy shows fate conspiring against Tess, making happiness impossible for her. From the moment of her setting out, her family has poorly equipped her to deal with the problems she faces. Hardy expresses early in the novel the sense of life's harshness and the doom that haunts Tess from the beginning to the end of her short and unhappy existence. He writes of her and her brothers and sisters as "captives," showing his view of their helplessness; they are captives first of their parents, but also of life, of fate:

> All these young souls were passengers in the Durbeyfield ship— entirely dependent on the judgment of the two Durbeyfield adults for their pleasures, their necessities, their health, even their existence. If the heads of the Durbeyfield household chose to sail into difficulty, disaster, starvation, disease, degradation, death, thither were these half-dozen little captives under hatches compelled to sail with them—six helpless creatures, who had never been asked if they wished for life on any terms, much less if they wished for it on such hard conditions as were involved in being of the shiftless house of Durbeyfield. (34)

Phrases such as "six helpless creatures" indicate Hardy's sense that these children have no control over their fate. From Hardy's point of view, all humans are children in the face of the forces shaping human life. And for Hardy these forces are usually destructive; they work against the ambitions, hopes, and dreams of humans, rather than with them. The Durbeyfield children represent common humanity as it sails into "difficulty, disaster, starvation, disease, degradation, death."

This use of a long quotation is justified by the student's extensive discussion of it (not only in the paragraphs provided here but throughout the entirety of the paper) as an expression of Hardy's pessimism. Hardy's pessimism is the kind of subtle and challenging concept that deserves the full and detailed illustration that the long quotation provides.

When you use a long quotation such as this, it should be relevant in its entirety, and you should spend considerable time discussing it, as this student has done. Certainly it is a mistake to dig out big chunks of quoted material, move them into your paper, and leave them there with little or no commentary. Such a procedure suggests padding.

SETTING QUOTATIONS INTO THE TEXT

Introducing the Quotation

Lead into your quotations. Tell your reader why you are offering the author's words that follow. Unless you prepare your readers, you leave them wondering, "Why did the writer quote this material? What step in the writer's argument is being demonstrated by this quotation?" Anticipate these questions and answer them as you lead into the quotation.

Commenting on the Quotation

Following the quotation, you often need to offer further commentary, especially if you want your readers to consider stylistic matters in the passage quoted. Here are paragraphs from a paper on Emily Dickinson that fails to connect its discussion, either before or after, with direct quotation:

STUDENT PARAGRAPHS

Emily Dickinson wrote frequently about death. Her poems look at death from many different points of view: from the point of view of the person looking forward to death, from the point of view of a dying person, from the point of view of someone who has long been dead. Her poems treat this subject in very specific terms. Often they include many details that surround the subject of death. These details make them more convincing.

> I heard a fly buzz when I died.
> The stillness in the room
> Was like the stillness in the air
> Between the heaves of storm.

Death can seem terrible or it can seem ordinary in her poems. There is a great variety in the moods and feelings.

This discussion includes valuable commentary and a relevant quotation, but the two have not been linked together. Has the quoted stanza been offered to demonstrate the use of details that make the poems convincing? To illustrate the way Dickinson's poems treat death from different points of view? To show that they include variety in moods and feelings? Since the author has not helped the reader by introducing the quotation or by offering any discussion of it afterward, the reader is justifiably perplexed and annoyed. It is as if the author suddenly decided, "It must be time to put a quote in my paper, so here's a quote." Having performed this duty, the author felt free to go on with the general discussion.

And notice how general this discussion is. It lacks ties to specific poems. Thus, while it offers some good insights, it wastes them because it fails to make them more than general and vague. They lack specific evidence, a lack made all the more obvious by the existence of the quotation. It is as if the author has failed to notice that he has an excellent piece of evidence right in front of his eyes.

The student who wrote this paragraph on Dickinson was encouraged to rewrite as follows:

REVISED STUDENT PARAGRAPHS

Emily Dickinson wrote frequently about death. Her poems look at death from different points of view, such as from the point of view of a person looking forward to death, in "Because I could not stop for Death, / He kindly stopped for me;" from the point of view of a dying person, as in "I heard a fly buzz when I died;" or from the point of view of someone who has long been dead, as in the final lines of "Because I could not stop for death":

> Since then, 'tis centuries, and yet
> Feels shorter than the day
> I first surmised the horses' heads
> Were toward eternity.

Her poems often treat death in specific terms by including small details that make the scene vivid and particular. For example, in the following poem she focuses on one small detail, a fly buzzing in the room. The focus on this small detail makes the poem memorable:

> I heard a fly buzz when I died.
> The stillness in the room
> Was like the stillness in the air
> Between the heaves of storm.

Death can seem terrible in her poems, or it can seem ordinary. In the poem above with its reference to the fly buzzing it seems ordinary, like a fact of life, as commonplace as a housefly, though the reference to the "heaves of storm" shows that great emotion has also been present during this death-bed scene.

This revised discussion not only is specific, it also has depth. As in many thoughtful revisions, the discussion grows in length because it digs deeper into the literature and because it introduces specific evidence. The revised discussion also takes a quantum leap upward in value. The paper has gone from a weak discussion, though full of promise, to an excellent analysis. Its promise has been fulfilled.

Identifying the Speaker of the Quotation

Make sure that your readers know exactly who is speaking the lines you are quoting. Notice the ambiguity in the following student paragraphs about Shakespeare's Macbeth:

STUDENT PARAGRAPHS

Macbeth and Lady Macbeth are both very ambitious and bloodthirsty. Yet while they are willing to commit violent crimes and murder to get what they want, they are also fearful at times, and this fear makes them hesitate to carry out their bloodthirsty plans:

> Alack, I am afraid they have awaked
> And 'tis not done! Th' attempt and not the deed
> Confounds us. Hark! I laid their daggers ready;
> He could not miss 'em. Had he not resembled
> My father as he slept, I had done 't.

This speech shows the intense fear that provides the atmosphere of the play. Macbeth and Lady Macbeth express this fear as well as cause it.

The author should indicate that Lady Macbeth speaks these lines. In addition, the author should provide a precise indication of the source of the quotation in the form of references to the act, scene, and line numbers. The absence of this information makes the paper vague in its use of quotations and undermines its authority.

Identifying the Author of Quoted Secondary Sources

If you quote from a secondary source, then identify the author and work when you introduce the quotation. It is best to put this information in the body of your paper rather than in a footnote or endnote, though such notes are acceptable in certain circumstances, such as in a research paper or a paper drawing on several sources. Once you have quoted from a secondary source, your subsequent quotations can be identified by the author's last name only and the page number in parentheses following the quotation. For example:

STUDENT PARAGRAPH

Macbeth is a complex character who combines good and evil, courage and fear, strengths and weaknesses. When Shakespeare introduces his audience to this ambiguous character, he brings into focus Macbeth's courage and skill as a soldier with words such as "brave Macbeth" and "valiant cousin" to show the respect others feel for him. But at the same time Shakespeare shows us an ambitious man ready to commit violent crime to gain power and a leader who can be ruthless and also fearful. According to Sylvan Barnet in his introduction to the Signet Classic edition of *Macbeth*, Macbeth's "first appearance on the stage . . . engages our sympathetic interest; he starts and seems 'to fear / Things that do sound so fair.' With hindsight we can say that he starts because he has already harbored criminal impulses that respond to the witches' words . . ." (xxx). Macbeth is like so many of Shakespeare's tragic heroes, a man of gigantic proportions who commits terrible crimes but one who also wins our sympathy. He is in "the company of sympathetic tragic heroes such as Hamlet and Romeo" (xxx).

There are three points to be noted in the use of the quotations above in addition to the full and accurate indication of the secondary source:

1. It makes use of three periods in the first portion of the quotation to indicate that words have been omitted from the original source (called *ellipses*) and does the same at the end.
2. It contains a *quotation within a quotation* and correctly puts the lines of verse quoted within the larger quotation inside single quotation marks and the larger quotation within double marks.
3. Since the quotation within the larger quotation is a fragment of verse, it indicates the break in lines with a slash (/), and it capitalizes the word following (*Things*) to indicate that it is the first word in the next line.

Setting Quotations into the Grammar of Your Sentences

Lead into your quotations and anchor them to your argument by setting them up as part of the grammar of your sentence. For example, the following sentence attempts to splice together the student's words with a quotation from Shakespeare, but in the process creates a new grammatically faulty sentence:

Although Macbeth is very ambitious to become king, he is uncertain how to gain the crown and hopes it will happen by, "chance will have me King, why, chance may crown me."

The grammar fails to work because in the student's sentence, *chance* is the object of the preposition *by*, whereas in Shakespeare's sentence, it is the subject of the verb. You avoid such problems if you keep in mind that your words and the quoted words must work together as a single sentence if they are run together grammatically. Notice how the following revisions offer alternative ways to solve the problem of the discordant grammar:

Revisions

1. Although Macbeth is very ambitious to become king, he is uncertain how to gain the crown and hopes that "If chance will have me King, why, chance may crown me" (1.3.143–144).
2. Although Macbeth is very ambitious to become king, he is uncertain how to gain the crown and hopes it will happen by chance. "If chance will have me King," he says in Act I, scene iii, "why, chance may crown me" (143–144).
3. Although Macbeth is very ambitious to become king, he is uncertain how to gain the crown and hopes it will happen by chance, as he expresses in the following lines:

> If chance will have me King, why,
>   chance may crown me,
> Without my stir. (1.3.143—144)

In the first revision, the student has run together his sentence with the quotation and blended the grammar. Notice that he needs no comma dividing his introductory words from the quotation because no comma is called for by the grammar of the sentence (the sentence created by the student's words plus the quotation). The second revision separates the introductory words in a complete sentence and treats the quotation as a separate sentence. The third revision also treats the quotation as grammatically separate and further separates it by its formatting. The third revision introduces the quotation with a colon, a common way to introduce an indented quotation (one set apart from text of the paper by wider margins and single spacing).

Each of these revisions is correct. Each indicates the source precisely. The third revision quotes Macbeth more fully and preserves the shape of the verse as it occurs on Shakespeare's page, and for this reason many English teachers would consider this the revision of choice.

Quoting One or Two Lines

Notice the way the following short quotation is set off by commas. The quotation has been run on or blended into the grammar of the student's sentence.

When Hamlet says to Ophelia, "Get thee to a nunnery," he is expressing his contempt for women's virtue.

Quoting Fragments

When you quote a fragment of a line you may not need any mark of punctuation preceding it. The following quotation requires no introductory punctuation, but it is followed by a comma because it forms part of an introductory adverbial clause. The sentence shows how the basis for punctuation at the beginning and end of quoted material grows from the grammar of the sentence in which it is embedded.

When Hamlet orders Ophelia "to a nunnery," he is expressing contempt for women's virtue.

Use of Periods to Indicate Ellipses

Ellipses is the omission of words from a direct quotation. Here is a revised version of the quotation from Thomas Hardy's *Tess of the d'Urbervilles* that uses ellipses rather than the full text:

All these young souls were passengers in the Durbeyfield ship . . . six helpless creatures, who had never been asked if they wished for life on any terms . . ." (34).

The three periods indicate the omissions, one from the middle of the quotation, one from the end.

When you offer an obvious fragment, you do not need the periods to indicate that it is torn from a longer text. Two examples:

Hamlet's questioning of life, asking "to be or not to be," shows both his restless mind and suicidal impulses.

Shakespeare's reference to Romeo and Juliet as a "pair of star-crossed lovers" expresses a foreshadowing of their doom.

Do *not* offer versions of the following mistaken punctuation:

When Hamlet orders Ophelia ". . . to a nunnery . . . ," he is expressing contempt for women's virtue.

Internal Punctuation

You must honor the punctuation as well as the words and spelling of your quoted author and leave the internal punctuation as you found it. Everything within the quotation marks except for the ending punctuation should be as the original author punctuated it. You change only the punctuation at the end of a quotation—for example, changing a comma to a period—to make it work with your sentence.

Long, Indented Quotations

As a rule, introduce long, indented quotations with a colon. The quotation then completes your sentence. Reexamine the long quotation from Hardy's *Tess of the d'Urbervilles* for the correct use of the colon to introduce indented quotations. Notice how the quotation finishes the student's sentence. A correct alternative would be for the student to use a period instead of a colon.

DOCUMENTING QUOTATIONS

Citing Your Sources

When you quote from a work of literature, you must be sure that your reader knows the source of the quotation. This means that your reader can turn to the page of the novel, the act or scene of the play, the lines of the poem you have quoted. Consider the problems posed by the following:

STUDENT PARAGRAPH

Dimmesdale is a hypocrite and a coward as we can see in the following quotation from Hawthorne: "He had been driven hither by the impulse of that Remorse which dogged him everywhere, and whose own sister and closely linked companion was that Cowardice which invariably drew him back." This shows that his cowardice always wins out over remorse. It makes his standing on the scaffold a vain show of expiation.

An initial problem arises from the lack of quotation marks to indicate that the final four words in the paragraph are a direct quotation. In addition, without any page references, the reader of this paper cannot know the exact source of the quotations included here. Indications of the source must include not just the page number, but also the edition of the work. The quotation above from Nathaniel Hawthorne's *The Scarlet Letter* might be from page 87 of one edition or page 120 of another. In fact, it was from page 1184 of the second edition of *The Norton Anthology of American Literature*, the text the student was using in conjunction with the rest of his class. Since it was the common text in the course, unless the instructor indicated otherwise, the student need not supply all of the publication information that would be included in a list of works cited for a research paper (i.e., such information as the date and place of publication). Here is how the student could have indicated the source:

REVISED STUDENT PARAGRAPH

Dimmesdale is a hypocrite and a coward as we can see in the following quotation from Hawthorne: "He had been driven hither by the impulse of that Remorse which dogged him everywhere, and whose own sister and closely linked companion was that Cowardice which invariably drew him back" (*Norton Anthology*, 2nd edition, vol. 1, 1184). This shows that his cowardice always wins out over remorse. This is why Hawthorne calls his standing on the scaffold a "vain show of expiation" (1184).

The student might have solved the problem of the source by providing a footnote after the first quotation indicating that all quotations in the paper can be found in *The Norton Anthology*. The note might read as follows:

All page references given in parentheses within the paper refer to pages of *The Norton Anthology of American Literature*, 2nd edition, Vol 1.

If you use a note like this, do not put a footnote after each quotation that follows. Instead provide the page numbers in parentheses right after the quotation, as the student has done in the second quotation from Hawthorne above. Notice that the student has not used anything but the naked numbers; there is no need to put "page" or "p." or "pp." This documentation procedure is formulated by the Modern Language Association, which sets the standards for publications on scholarly topics in the field of English.

Using a List of Works Cited

Because the student quoting from *The Norton Anthology* above was citing a work the whole class was using and which therefore his teacher and his readers knew, the indication of the source would cause no difficulty. However, if the student cited as a source a text not being used in class, he should give full publication information at the end of the paper in a list of "Works Cited." This is especially important if the paper includes references to several works, among them secondary sources. Lists of works cited can also be called a "Bibliography," important especially for research papers. To learn the correct form for a bibliography, consult a guide to research papers in English literature.

Exceptions to the Requirement to Cite Sources

The exceptions to specifying the source occur when you are writing on a work of literature or a passage from it that is easily identified, such as Hamlet's "To be or not to be" soliloquy. Or possibly your teacher has assigned a quotation for you to discuss, or a scene from a play, or a passage or chapter from a work of fiction. In such cases, the sources of your quotations will be obvious and require no further references. For examples of quotations from poetry that need no page citations, turn back to the student paragraphs on Emily Dickinson. The poems quoted are short and easily identified by the lines, allowing readers to turn to the sources with no difficulty.

Avoiding Footnotes by the Use of Parentheses

Most English teachers believe that references to the source of quotations are best kept simple. Footnotes and endnotes are not simple, at least not for most of us, and you should avoid them if you can. You will need them in a research paper or a study citing many different sources, but the usual English course paper asking you to discuss a single work of literature does not demand such notes. Instead, indicate your sources in the body of your paper and bury the information about page and line numbers in parentheses following the quotation, as has been done throughout this guide.

Citing a Play

When quoting from a play with numbered lines, you can refer to act and scene and line numbers. This is commonly done in referring to Shakespeare's plays, as we see in the following sample:

Hamlet expresses his awareness of his own over-reliance on thought at the expense of action when he says, "And thus the native hue of resolution / Is sicklied o'er with the pale cast of thought" (3.1.84,85).

The numbers in parentheses tell the reader that the quotation comes from Act 3, Scene 1, lines 84 and 85. Since the student's sentence makes it clear that the quotation is from Shakespeare's *Hamlet*, the student needs no reference to the author or title.

Citing a Poem

References to poems often use line numbers. If the poem is long, there may be divisions within it that you should refer to, such as the book numbers in Homer's *The Odyssey*. Notice how the student of the following commentary on Walt Whitman's *Song of Myself* indicates that his reference is to line, not page numbers:

In *Song of Myself*, Whitman's positive attitude toward death is part of his acceptance of all the stages and facts of life:

Has anyone supposed it lucky to be born?
I hasten to inform him or her it is just as lucky to die, and I know it.
I pass death with the dying and birth with the new-washed babe and am not contain'd between my hat and boots. (lines 131–134)

Citing Secondary Sources

Most of the citations in this chapter so far have been from the primary texts, meaning the works of literature you are studying. When citing secondary sources, you must take care to indicate all of your borrowing and provide full information so that your readers can track down your sources. If you fail to do this you run the risk of being charged with plagiarism. In the following example, the student indicates clearly in parentheses how he has drawn on a secondary source:

STUDENT PARAGRAPH

Critics often point out that Conrad's *Heart of Darkness* exposes "the infinite capacities for reversion and crime" found in "the unconscious mind of each of us" (Albert J. Guerard, "Introduction," *Heart of Darkness & Secret Sharer*, Signet Editions, 9). The character of Kurtz in particular embodies Conrad's sense of criminal potentialities that lurk in the hearts of all people, black or white. Because of Kurtz's greed for ivory and his "moral deterioration and reversion to savagery" (Guerard, 13), the Chief of the Inner Station becomes symbolic of all the European evil exploitation of the native Africans.

Punctuation of References in Parentheses

In the examples of references in parentheses cited above, notice that the final period that closes the first quotation goes outside the parentheses. The comma after the second quotation also follows the parentheses.

PARAPHRASING INSTEAD OF QUOTING

Using Your Own Words to Paraphrase

You paraphrase an author when you put the argument of the text you are paraphrasing into your own words. Notice that in paraphrasing, the words are your own but the ideas are borrowed. As in using quotations, paraphrasing demands that you indicate the source of your borrowing. Failure to document the source of the material you have paraphrased is a form of plagiarism.

Indicate the sources of your paraphrasing just as you would the source of your quotations, with references in parentheses. Suppose, for example, that instead of quoting directly from Guerard's introduction to Conrad's *Heart of Darkness* you decided to paraphrase his argument. Here is a way to indicate the borrowing without the use of a footnote or endnote:

In his introduction to *Heart of Darkness*, Albert Guerard points out how the story expresses the way humans revert to savage and criminal conduct when they return as Kurtz does to the primitive jungle. Then atavistic criminal tendencies usually repressed in the unconscious rise to the surface and turn men toward savagery (Albert J. Guerard, "Introduction," *Heart of Darkness & Secret Sharer*, Signet Editions, 9).

Using Paraphrase to Summarize

Paraphrasing is especially useful when you want to summarize the argument of a chapter or of several pages. It is a way of avoiding the use of long quotations that might swamp your writing. It is also helpful in summarizing the argument of a secondary source.

6

ORGANIZATION

- Developing a Writing Strategy
- The Scratch Outline
- Student Scratch Outline & Examination Essay
- Explication
- Methods of Development
- Drawing Up an Outline
- Outlining on a Computer
- The Five-Paragraph Essay

DEVELOPING A WRITING STRATEGY

A Writing Strategy as a Large-Scale Plan

Once you have selected a topic for your literary essay, you must decide how you will present it. For this you need a writing strategy. Think of your strategy as a large-scale plan that shapes the entire paper. An effective strategy grows from your comprehensive understanding of all aspects of what you are trying to accomplish: your subject, your thesis (if you have one), your purpose, and your audience. It's a view from a mountaintop of the entire terrain you mean to cover.

A Thesis as Part of the Writing Strategy

If you have come up with a thesis to defend, you have already made a decision about your writing strategy, since a thesis is part of your approach. The need to explain the thesis, demonstrate its validity, and support it with evidence dictates to a certain extent what form your paper will take.

Assignments that Dictate Your Writing Strategy

Your thesis may at times be dictated or suggested by your assignment, as it is in the following assignments:

- "Write a 500- to 800-word paper on Emily Dickinson's conception of nature as a source of poetic inspiration."
- "Discuss the importance of the setting in Emily Brontë's *Wuthering Heights*."

Both of these topics point you toward a thesis and to a certain extent suggest an organizational approach. But they provide just the beginning; to do a good job with either of these assignments you would need to come up with a clear and limited thesis and then decide how to present the material to support it.

Some assignments push you even further toward a writing strategy and an organizational plan. Consider the following assignment on Shakespeare's *Hamlet*:

- "Write a comparison and contrast of Hamlet and Laertes, showing how they are alike in situation and character, and how they differ. Consider their attitudes toward the loss of their fathers and the revenge they want for this loss, and compare the ways they go about gaining revenge."

Obviously this assignment forces on you a comparison-and-contrast paper. A topic such as this is often set as an essay on an examination because it forces the student to discuss certain facts and reveals the extent of the student's understanding. The topic might serve equally well for a paper written outside of class, in which case you can see that the steps that have been taken to narrow the topic and to establish an organizing strategy are those you want to take on your own when writing on a large and complex work such as Shakespeare's *Hamlet*.

Writing an Examination Essay

Much of your writing on literature is accomplished in class as tests and examinations. Typically your instructions for writing narrow the topic and provide the beginning of a thesis for your examination essays. Nevertheless, as a rule you need to organize your thoughts and information before you launch into your essay. Students vary greatly in their ability to write under the pressure of time. Chief among the abilities you want to develop to perform well on essay examinations is organizational dexterity. Even if your time is sharply limited, you want to spend a few moments putting your thoughts and knowledge into logical order. Perhaps especially when you write against a deadline you need a strategy that is written down in some kind of plan, however sketchy.

A first step toward a writing strategy is an outline. Obviously you do not have time for a formal outline when the clock is ticking, but you will find that you save yourself time in the long run if you at least draw up a scratch outline, a quick plan that helps you to develop coherence in your essay.

THE SCRATCH OUTLINE

A scratch outline amounts to the bare minimum of organization. You begin a scratch outline with a thesis statement, possibly stated in fragmentary form. Then you quickly put down the main points you want to cover that will support your thesis—maybe two to five points. Next you introduce the evidence that will support your main points—quotations or specific references to the literary work. Finally you write a conclusion.

Look at the following essay topic and the scratch outline that the student used to prepare her essay. The student was allowed to use her text in writing her essay, so before she began writing she was able to dig out some direct quotations, which she included in her outline.

• *Topic for a 40-minute essay:* "According to William Lloyd Garrison, 'Slavery has a natural, an inevitable tendency to brutalize every noble faculty of man.' Drawing on *The Autobiography of Frederick Douglass*, develop Garrison's statement into a well-organized essay. Consider the brutalizing effects of slavery not only on the slaves but on the rest of the population. Be specific. You may use your text to find supporting quotations."

STUDENT SCRATCH OUTLINE & EXAMINATION ESSAY ON *THE AUTOBIOGRAPHY OF FREDERICK DOUGLASS*

STUDENT SCRATCH OUTLINE

Thesis: Slavery erodes (1) intelligence, (2) humanity, (3) morality of both master and slave.
   1. intelligence: thinking discouraged in slaves. "a still tongue makes a wise head" (1889). reading forbidden. "It was unlawful, as well as unsafe, to teach a slave to read" (1895).
   2. morality of slaves: stealing justified, drinking and promiscuity common, family life weak.
   3. morality of masters: cruelty, hardness, adultery, murder. "Under its influence, the tender heart turned to stone, and the lamb-like disposition gave way to one of tigerlike fierceness" (1897).
   Conclusion: toll on generations who are only now recovering.

STUDENT EXAMINATION ESSAY

Slavery, the Brutalization of Humans

Slavery, the subjection of a class of humans to the rule of another class, is as degrading to the masters as it is to the slaves. It goes against the very nature of humans to be so inhumane as to force another into servitude. The institution of slavery erodes the intelligence, humanity, and morality of both master and slave.

The intelligence of the slaves is the most obvious evidence of decay. Slaves were discouraged from offering opinions and even from thinking. In his autobiography, Douglass noted that slaves had learned "that a still tongue makes a wise head" (1889). Reading was forbidden, as it was feared that educated slaves would be discontent slaves. "It was unlawful, as well as unsafe, to teach a slave to read" (1895). So intelligence became the first victim of slavery.

Slavery had an effect on the morality of slaves, and actions that would have been considered unlawful became accepted by the slave population. Stealing food was justified by the slaves as being an exchange of the master's goods, from one form to another. Drinking was a great pastime in the winter free period, and slaves annually became rowdy and inebriated. Promiscuity increased, because the slaves were no longer allowed to be married, and thus had no spouse to be faithful to. This moral decay occurred because there was no reward in being an honest slave; it would not feed you, comfort you, or make you feel good about yourself, because you were a slave, the lowest form of human life.

The belief that slaves were the lowest form of human life was fostered by the masters, who encouraged slaves to believe it. The masters' moral code also suffered as a result of slavery. "Under its influence, the tender heart turned to stone, and the lamb-like disposition gave way to one of tigerlike fierceness" (1897). Slaves were whipped like animals, fed like pigs, and worked like horses. The aristocratic, "genteel" Southerners became driving masters, and hired the cruelest of overseers for their human beasts. These men who put their Southern wives on a pedestal thought nothing of breaking a sacred commandment with a slave. Not only did these "religious men" commit adultery, they also committed murder. And by far the greatest indicator of the extent to which slavery had eroded the moral fiber of society was that their crimes went unpunished. At a time when the merest unpleasant word could earn a slave a whipping that would take him to the brink of death, murderous masters went unpunished.

There is no greater injustice than slavery, no greater cruelty. It has taken its toll on the hearts, minds, and souls of generations. Only now are the victims of slavery, the decedents of the original slaves, recovering intelligence, morality, humanity, and justice.

Incompleteness & Repetition as Failures to Plan

If you don't begin with a large-scale plan and a sense of strategy, you may wander in your attempt to develop your ideas, failing to cover some of the ground that is essential to your argument and needlessly repeating ideas instead of developing them. Incompleteness and repetition are common problems in writing papers on literary topics, and they are often symptoms that the writer proceeded without a formal plan or writing strategy. Other common symptoms of inadequate planning are the absence of paragraphing, disjointed thinking, and lack of clarity.

Simple Writing Strategy: Journal Writing

To look at a simple example of how strategy relates to your subject, your purpose, and your audience, think of a brief journal entry. To write a first-person reflection in a single paragraph you need little planning. Your strategy may be no more than a decision simply to express your first reactions to a work of literature. You may begin with your initial response or the first idea that comes to you and proceed to record whatever pops into your mind in the order it comes to you. An example of such writing follows. It is a brief journal response about the return of Odysseus to his native island of Ithaka in Homer's *The Odyssey*.

STUDENT JOURNAL ENTRY

Odysseus arrives on the island of Ithaka and has no sense of where he is at first. Then he meets Athena and she points out to him the landmarks of his homeland. Together they plan a strategy for his return to his manor and his defeat of the suitors. Athena tells Odysseus that she will disguise him as a beggar so that he can find out what is happening in his manor and learn who are the loyal servants. The disguise will also allow him to get into his kingdom unobserved, like a spy, and avoid the fate of Agamemnon. The use of a disguise is typical of Odysseus and Athena. It reminds me of how he invaded the city of Troy in the belly of a wooden horse, and of how he called himself Nohbdy when he was with Polyphemos, the one-eyed Kyklops, and later took the disguise of a ram to escape the cave. It's a good example of how tricky Odysseus can be and of how he likes to use an alias or a mask or some other deception. He seems to enjoy deceiving people. When he first met up with Athena on Ithaka he told her a typical lie about who he was. She saw right through the lie, of course, since she seems to know everything about Odysseus, but she also congratulated him for his effort. This is a man who does not like to reveal himself to anyone on a first meeting, maybe because he never knows who might end up being his enemy.

This writing on Odysseus, like much journal work, is exploratory and proceeds according to no predetermined plan. Notice the way it moves back and forth in time, shifting from the arrival of Odysseus on Ithaka back to his earlier adventures, then returning to the scene on Ithaka. This rambling works fine in a journal entry but would seem too unplanned and informal in a paper developing a thesis.

Now consider the following assignment to the same student:

• "Discuss the return of Odysseus to Ithaka and the reasons he uses the disguise of a beggar."

To write this paper, the student began with the journal entry above and went on to create the following outline:

STUDENT OUTLINE

    I. Problems Odysseus faces when he returns to Ithaka.
       A. Suitors: They might attack and kill Odysseus. Compare with Agamemnon.
       B. Servants: Many disloyal, might side with suitors, join in attack against Odysseus. Example: Melanthios, the goatherd.
       C. Family: Could also be disloyal.
   II. Disguise and Deception as Solutions to the Problems.
       A. Odysseus can spy on suitors, work out plans for attack.
       B. Odysseus can observe servants off guard.
       C. Odysseus can test his family's hospitality.
  III. Melanthios: disloyal servant compared with Eumaios.
  IV. Antinoos and the suitors: lack of hospitality and outright hostility.
   V. Telemakhos and Penelope: loyal and hospitable.

Using the outline as a guide, the student wrote the following paper. Notice how its greater complexity compared with the original journal entry requires this greater degree of planning and organization. The paper uses a cause-and-effect argument: Because Odysseus wants to avoid certain dangers, he is disguised as a beggar with certain results. A cause-and-effect argument, like any argument, requires logical steps if it is to be orderly and convincing. These logical steps are indicated in the outline and argued in the paper with supporting examples.

STUDENT PAPER

Odysseus as a Beggar

When Odysseus returns to Ithaka in Book 13 of *The Odyssey,* he must be very careful because his life is in danger. To return home as himself and enter his home proclaiming to all that he, the mighty Odysseus, has returned would probably result in his being killed at the hands of the suitors. At several points in *The Odyssey* Homer introduces the story of Agamemnon, who returned home from Troy after a long absence. When he arrived at his palace, Agamemnon was unaware that his wife had taken a lover, turned against him, and planned to kill him. Odysseus has this danger in the back of his mind. He says to Athena, "An end like Agamemnon's / might very likely have been mine, a bad end, / bleeding to death in my own hall" (lines 482–484). In addition, he knows his servants might have joined forces with the suitors and want to kill him, as he sees when he meets up with Melanthios. A final danger might come from his own family, which was the source of the danger for Agamemnon.

Athena is aware of all these problems; therefore, she transforms Odysseus into a beggar. "Now, for a while, I shall transform you; / not a soul will know you" (lines 499–500) she says to him. This way he can enter his manor unknown to all, just the way he entered Troy unsuspected in the belly of the wooden horse. The suitors will be caught off guard, and Odysseus can obtain his sweet revenge and let black death fall upon each one. As a beggar he can discover the real truth about his servants, which would be impossible if he returned home in his true form. At the same time he can see how his wife is behaving with the suitors. For all he knows, she may have taken one of the suitors as a lover and be ready to kill him. He can see as well if his wife and son are hospitable according to the religious beliefs of the Greeks and are willing to take in a poor beggar.

A good example of the success of the beggar's disguise comes when Odysseus is making his way to his manor with Eumaios. They meet the goatherd, Melanthios, leading a string of goats to be slaughtered for the suitors' feasting. Melanthios is extremely rude to Odysseus, calls him a "pig," a "stinking beggar," and "a licker of pots" (Book 17, lines 280–281), and then kicks him. Odysseus knows from that point on that Melanthios cannot be trusted, that he has gone over to the side of the suitors. Another example of the effectiveness of the disguise occurs when Odysseus goes into the manor to beg for food from the suitors. Here he discovers that Antinoos, the aristocratic leader of the suitors, won't give him even a crust of bread. Antinoos says, "What evil wind blew in this pest?" (Book 17, line 85), and is so inhospitable that he throws a stool at the old beggar. Ironically it is Antinoos who is the one who blew in on an evil wind.

On the other hand, Odysseus discovers through his disguise that Penelope and Telemakhos are still loyal to him and have not gone over to the suitors' side. They also follow the religious codes of the Greeks in being kind to the beggar and offering him hospitality. So even though his worst fears about his family did not come true, the disguise was helpful in letting Odysseus see the truth about his wife and son. This might have made him feel even closer to them after he was reunited with them.

EXPLICATION

Using the Organization of the Work of Literature as a Guide

Papers that explain the meaning of a brief work, such as a sonnet, or explore the significance of a small section of a larger work—a minor character, the significance of a symbol, or a brief scene—can often use the organization of the literature as the guide to writing. With a poem, for example, you can begin your analysis with the first lines and work your way through the poem, allowing the poet's organization to become yours. Such is the case in the following discussion of Shakespeare's Sonnet 73. This writing is *explication*, which means literally "an unfolding." In literary explication, what is being unfolded is the meaning, which in poetic form is often obscure or packed into metaphors and symbolic language.

STUDENT PAPER

Shakespeare's Sonnet 73

Shakespeare's Sonnet 73 is a poem about the poet's old age and approaching death. It begins in the first quatrain with images from the end of fall, the season of dying. The poet compares himself to "yellow leaves" and "boughs which shake against the cold," bleak pictures of the coming of winter. Then he offers a comparison of the tree limbs to "bare ruined choirs, where late the sweet birds sang" which intensifies the sense of desolation because it brings in the loss of something sweet and beautiful.

In the next quatrain the poet compares his old age to the twilight of the day. He says he is like a fading sunset, and he looks forward to the coming night "that seals up all in rest." The night is called "death's second self," the first mention of the word *death*, which introduces the idea of the poet's approaching death.

In the third quatrain the poem introduces the image of a fire that is going out. The fire is being choked by ashes, which are called "the ashes of his youth." It is as if the poet were saying that he is old and gray and like ashes. It can remind the reader of the "ashes to ashes, dust to dust" that symbolize human death. This third quatrain mentions the "death-bed," which deepens the gloom and intensifies the image of the poet's coming death.

The three quatrains create a very gloomy mood. Through the images of the dying year, the dying day, and the dying fire, the reader understands how sad and depressed the poet feels. He is old and dying, and he knows his life is about over. But then he thinks of his lover and he feels uplifted, because he believes his lover will feel even more strongly for him since they must soon be separated. The knowledge of the poet's approaching death "makes thy love more strong," he says. In this way the poem ends with a strong affirmation of their shared love. The melancholy tone of the three quatrains is not exactly denied, but it is shown to be just part of the poet's response. The final response is more positive and shows the strength of love, a common theme in many of Shakespeare's sonnets.

In this example of explication, the entire paper is devoted to unfolding the meaning of the sonnet. The organizational strategy is simple and straightforward.

More often explication serves as part of a paper. It is a common procedure in writing about literature, because in order to support a thesis or argue a point you must often explain the meaning of certain lines of poetry, a passage from a novel, a symbol or recurring image. This points to the way literary papers often make use of several different kinds of writing. Different kinds of writing are essentially different ways of developing your thought and argument. Some of these ways to develop and organize the argument of literary papers are discussed here:

METHODS OF DEVELOPMENT

Explication

Explication is illustrated in the preceding discussion of Shakespeare's Sonnet 73.

Analysis

You make use of analysis when you break something into its component parts and show the relationship among the parts. As an example, let's say you are writing a paper on the pattern of imagery in Shakespeare's *Hamlet*. You want to break apart several of the speeches to show images of poison and sickness. Your analysis would include digging out these images and showing their repetition throughout the play, the way the images build up an overall pattern, and the effect of this pattern of imagery on the mood of the play.

Exemplification

When you use exemplification, you provide examples from the literature that support your thesis or argument. These examples generally take the form of references to the text, such as to the actions and statements of characters in a play, to the language of a poem, or to the setting of a story. In addition, direct quotation provides an essential aspect of exemplification. Exemplification occurs in nearly all well-developed literary papers.

Classification

Using classification, you put literary works or aspects of literary works into categories. Dividing plays into tragedies and comedies is an obvious example of classification. You might want to show how Shakespeare's *Hamlet* fits into the category of revenge tragedy, in what ways James Joyce's *A Portrait of the Artist as a Young Man* belongs among the novels of adolescent development, or how Emily Dickinson's poems belong among the Romantics. Notice that in order to support your classifications you would probably need to use analysis, explication, and comparison and contrast, among other strategies of development.

Definition

You use definition frequently in literary papers to state the meaning of a term or concept or to identify the characteristics of something. Let's say that you want to call the character Pip from Charles Dickens' *Great Expectations* a romantic hero. In order to make your thesis clear, you need to define the term *romantic* and possibly as well the term *hero.* Definition is essential to literary papers whenever you use abstract terms such as *romantic* and *romanticism, realist* and *realism, idealist, conservative,* or any other that encompasses multiple dictionary definitions.

Definition rarely provides the development for an entire paper. It is frequently important early in a paper to provide the meanings you will build on throughout your argument. For example, if you want to discuss William Wordsworth as a nature writer, you might open your paper with your working definition of the term *nature.*

Cause & Effect

If you set out to demonstrate that Pip's introduction to Miss Havisham and Estella in *Great Expectations* causes profound changes in his character such as his desire to become a gentleman, you would organize your paper using a cause-and-effect argument. Arguing from causes to effects is fundamental to human reasoning and shows up in many different kinds of writing. It has a scientific, objective quality to it and works best when you take the time to organize your thinking carefully. To argue a cause-and-effect thesis, you need to take care in providing convincing evidence as well as in organizing the steps in your thinking.

To appreciate some of the challenges of cause-and-effect argument, imagine you want to demonstrate that the appearance of the ghost in Shakespeare's *Hamlet* causes the young prince to go mad. To make a convincing case, you must demonstrate that in fact Hamlet is mad, or at least mad at certain moments, which will require careful organizing and thinking as well as convincing evidence. Then you must trace this effect back to its origins and demonstrate that the ghost, and not a host of other possible causes (such as his father's death and his mother's remarriage), has turned Hamlet's wits. Within the play several characters argue this point. Polonius, for example, expresses to the king his belief that Hamlet's mental disturbances are caused by his unrequited love for Ophelia, but Claudius disagrees and advances a different view, doubting that Hamlet is in fact mad.

The points to be made from these conflicting views about Hamlet's madness are that cause-and-effect argument, although often very attractive to the human mind, can provide a number of challenges in reasoning and therefore in writing, and that successful handling of a cause-and-effect argument demands considerable planning and organizing. It is one thing to toss off statements about causes, and another to build a convincing case that shows certain effects growing from certain causes. There is the story of the boy out for a walk in a park with his mother on a windy day. Annoyed by the wind, he complains to his mother, "If they cut down all these trees, we wouldn't have this terrible wind." Causes are often not what they seem to be, and just as the causes of certain sickness have eluded medical science, so too have the causes of a number of literary uncertainties, such as the reasons for Hamlet's delay in taking his revenge. In short, if you take up this line of reasoning in a literary paper, do so armed with logic and evidence plus a recognition of their limits and the limits of the human mind.

Argumentation & Persuasion

You will often want to support your thesis with argumentation and persuasion. When you argue a case, you attempt to prove logically that a particular view is correct or that your reading of a literary work is accurate and superior to other readings. Your argument may make use of cause-and-effect reasoning, explication, analysis, and other methods of literary discussion. Like many of the methods of presenting ideas and observations, argumentation and persuasion are rarely the only ones used in a paper. Many teachers feel that any paper with a thesis uses an argumentative approach, since much of the paper will be devoted to advancing the thesis and offering arguments in its defense. In any case, persuasion is most effective when it is orderly. Take time to organize your argument carefully, which means outlining the logic of your thinking and finding evidence for each step.

Comparison & Contrast

Like cause and effect, comparison and contrast is a fundamental way the human mind works. You will find that comparison and contrast is relevant for many different literary assignments, in part because works of literature often make use of the technique. We write papers comparing Hamlet and Laertes because Shakespeare wrote a play comparing the two. They are character foils, and a paper contrasting the two can go a long way toward an understanding of each of them and of the play. The same may be said of

Romeo and Mercutio, of Ismene and Antigone, of Teiresias and Oedipus, of Huck Finn and Tom Sawyer. The creative mind and the critical mind both move forward by finding similarities and differences.

Each of the above comparisons arise within a single work. Comparison and contrast is often an excellent way to bring two or more literary works together. Whenever you attempt to cover two or more literary works in a single paper, you need to invest special care in organization. For this reason, there follows a sample outline of a way to organize comparison-and-contrast papers. The outline applies to a comparison and contrast of Pip from Charles Dickens' *Great Expectations* and Janie from Zora Neale Hurston's *Their Eyes Were Watching God*. Notice that the outline points to a running comparison which has the writer and reader moving back and forth between the two works. This avoids the problems that arise when a student decides to discuss one work and one-half of the comparison in the first part of the paper and the second work and the second half of the comparison in the second half of the paper, thus dividing the paper in two.

1. First similarity: youth and inexperience of the world
   a. Pip
   b. Janie
2. Second similarity: poverty and low social status
   a. Pip
   b. Janie
3. Third similarity: family background
   a. Pip
   b. Janie
4. First difference: gender
   a. Pip
   b. Janie
5. Second difference: marriage
   a. Pip
   b. Janie

DRAWING UP AN OUTLINE

Approaches to outlining are as individual as anything else in writing. What form your outline takes, when in the writing process you draw it up, and whether you use one at all, depend in part on what you are writing and what kind of a writer you are. Brief papers and in-class examinations call for a scratch outline; longer, comprehensive topics require a careful, formal outline that you may need to revise several times as you work on your paper.

Some students hate outlining and skip the step altogether. Most professional writers use outlines, and many of them consider outlining an essential step in creating an orderly expository essay. If you have resisted outlining but have noticed that your instructors frequently comment on the disorder of your papers and the lack of coherence in your arguments, it's time for outlining to become a part of your writing life. There is no doubt you will improve your chances of writing a coherent paper if you make the effort to outline before your write. Any outline is better than none. It has been said of playing a hand of bridge, a poor plan is better than no plan. The same can be said of writing a literary paper.

The Formal Outline

A formal outline is highly organized and logical with a place for thesis, main points, supporting points, details, and conclusion. Here is a common version of a formal outline:

Thesis Statement
I. First Main Idea
    A. First Subordinate Point
    B. Second Subordinate Point
        1. First Supporting Detail
        2. Second Supporting Detail
            a. First Minor Point
            b. Second Minor Point
                i. First Supporting Detail
                ii. Second Supporting Detail
II. Second Main Idea
III. Third Main Idea
    A. First Subordinate Point
    B. Second Subordinate Point
IV. Fourth Main Idea

Notice how main ideas are indicated with Roman numerals, subordinate points or ideas with capital letters, then supporting details and minor points with Arabic numerals and lower-case letters and finally lower-case Roman numerals. Many writers quickly become impatient with formal outlines and refuse to use all outlines because of their distaste for the formal version. If you find yourself in this group, try coming up with your own outlining plan. Anything that gets your ideas and points down in an orderly fashion as a preliminary plan will help you to write a clearer paper.

Sentence Outlines

Sentence outlines are formal outlines that require the use of grammatically complete sentences punctuated with a period at the end. They are useful in that they encourage you to make complete statements on your topic at this planning stage. In writing your paper you will find that you can often incorporate many if not all of these sentences. Sentence outlines encourage you to say something specific about your topic at the outline stage.

Item Outlines

Item outlines use words and phrases and are quicker to draw up than sentence outlines. An item outline resembles a table of contents. It indicates the topics to be covered but says little about the topics. Often writers use terms such as *Introduction* and *Conclusion* in item outlines, showing the vagueness of this form of planning compared with sentence outlines. If you use an item outline, avoid using as complete items such terms as *Introduction* that refer to your organization rather than to your topic. Instead, enlarge your outline so that your item includes information about your topic, such as "Introduction: Romeo's Emotional Nature shown in Act I" as the first item in a character analysis of Romeo. Note that this item introduces not only the character to be discussed and a description of him (his "emotional nature"), but it also includes an indication of what part of the literary work will be examined. You can see how much more help such an expanded discussion will give you than the one word *Introduction*.

OUTLINING ON A COMPUTER

Many computer programs have outlining capabilities. These programs set up the indentations and number and letter the headings automatically. Outlining programs may allow you to view your writing as text and outline at the same time in two different windows. Changes in your text cause changes in the outline, and changes in your outline create changes in your text; with two-way viewing or a split screen you can view them both at once. Also you may be able to hide text. The hidden text is usually in the form of notes you make for your own guidance as you write, which are not printed unless you specifically command your computer to do so.

When you create an outline on a computer, print the outline before you write the first draft so that you can have the outline at your elbow as a guide. Even though you can move back to the outline on the screen, you need a printed copy. A printed outline is easier to follow and can be viewed in its entirety.

With a computer-generated outline you may make use of different type sizes and styles to help you organize your material visually. For example, you might use bold printing for main points to help them stand out, and you might want to enlarge the print for major points.

THE FIVE-PARAGRAPH ESSAY

Many teachers of literature require their students to use a five-paragraph structure for their formal essays, and many students find the five-paragraph essay to be a helpful way to organize their material. Typically a five-paragraph essay begins with an introduction that states the thesis and the three points that will support the thesis. It then develops the three points, each point in a separate paragraph. It concludes with a summary that reviews the points and the thesis.

Objections to this five-paragraph strategy point to its predictable and mechanical qualities. Since the introductory paragraph summarizes the points to follow, the three middle paragraphs of development lack a sense of exploration and discovery. The concluding paragraph often amounts to little more than repetition. If you are attracted to this five-paragraph essay because of its predictable and orderly qualities, keep in mind its limitations and try to invest your writing with freshness and originality so that your essay does not seem a mechanical fulfilling of a formula with dutiful repetitions of points and conclusions.

For an example of a five-paragraph essay used effectively, refer back to the examination essay on Frederick Douglass and slavery at the beginning of this chapter.

7

THE ROUGH DRAFT

- **Rough Drafts as Rehearsals**
- **Planning Your Time**
- **Writing Rapidly**
- **First Drafts on the Computer**
- **The Second Draft**
- **Dividing Your Rough Draft into Sections**

ROUGH DRAFTS AS REHEARSALS

There are students who sit down and write a single draft of a paper and submit it as the final work. The odds of writing a good paper without putting it through rough drafts resemble the odds of playing a good varsity game without any practices, or performing a polished musical recital without any rehearsals. Look on rough drafts as rehearsals. You need them to develop some idea of what you want to say and how you want to say it.

Rough drafts are tentative. They provide you with the opportunity to explore your topic and to discover your own thoughts on the literature you are studying. They give you time to take risks and make mistakes. The sentence you write first in a rough draft need not be the opening sentence of the final paper. It does not need to be a good sentence or even a complete sentence. Look on the first words you put down as sparks to get the fire going.

Ignoring the Editor in You

As you launch into the draft, don't fuss with wording or sentence structure. Don't allow yourself to become self-conscious, fearful of what your readers will say of these words. There is a time for this concern with the impression your paper makes, but it comes at a later stage. The attention to the final appearance of your paper belongs to the editor in you, not the writer of rough drafts. If the editor intrudes now with demands for correct grammar, judicious word choices, and neat format, you will feel paralysis. Writer's block seizes hold of us when we allow the editor in us to control the creative scribbler. Rough drafts belong to the creative scribbler. Let the scribbler go to this scribbling without restraint.

PLANNING YOUR TIME

Preparing to Write the Rough Draft

Everything you have done so far in the form of prewriting—selecting a topic, defining your thesis, selecting quotations—amounts to your preparations for writing the rough draft, but in addition to these steps you need to plan the first drafting session carefully. Your preparations should include the following:

• *Plan your time.* Set a schedule for yourself. The best schedule accommodates your own writing preferences. Do you work best in the morning? In the evening? Early in the evening? Do you work best in long sessions—an hour-and-a-half to two hours—or in a series of short sessions of 20 or 30 minutes each? Your schedule may need to accommodate external conditions. Perhaps you have a couple of roommates who are noisy in the late afternoon, or you live in a dormitory that is at its quietest in the morning hours. Most writers, even the most disciplined, find it difficult to compete with distractions and noise. Give yourself the benefit of the quietest conditions you can find.

• *Write well in advance of the due date.* Obviously if you begin work on an important paper at 10:30 the night before it is due you have put yourself at an enormous disadvantage. Major papers require several work sessions. You improve your chances of writing a good paper if you allow time to work on your paper in stages. This applies to all stages in the process of writing, and it applies to the draft itself. The longer the paper the more it will benefit from several sessions at the drafting stage. When you finish with a draft, you increase your editorial sharpness in detecting its faults if you can put the paper aside for a day or two.

• *Arrange your work space.* Many writers are as fussy about where they work as about when. Do you have access to a writing center, for example, where the conditions are favorable? Or do you like doing your work tucked away in a corner of your own room surrounded by familiar possessions and your books?

• *Assemble your resources.* Before you begin, gather your dictionary, notebooks, texts, pens, and pencils. You should have the primary text—the poem or story or play you are discussing—open on your desk next to you.

• *Have the following at your elbow:*

- outline
- quotations
- prewriting documents
- notes

Review all these materials before you begin the draft. Return to them frequently during your drafting sessions.

The Worst-Case Writing Scenario

We all know how to make difficult work even more resistant—forget about planning. The very worst experiences in writing look like this: You sit down to write with little idea what you want to say and with no plans. "I'll just wing it," you say, knowing that your writing wings are anything but sturdy. But the paper is due at 8:00 the next morning, so what can you do? You stare for five minutes at the blank screen or blank sheet of paper. Nothing comes to you. Five minutes turn to 10, to 15, to half an hour, then an hour. In that time you have managed to write two or three irrelevant sentences that go nowhere, so you get rid of them. The emptiness of the page or screen glares back at you. There are distractions everywhere, and you can't resist any of them. "Forget it," you finally say getting up from your desk. "I'll do my calculus first and come back to this paper at eleven."

Does anyone need this scenario played out to its bitter end? We've all gone through this valley of ashes. No doubt Shakespeare and Hemingway knew it well. Experienced writers all have similar advice to avoid repeated trips through this valley: Plan your work. If you sit down armed with time, an outline, some quotations, a thesis, and some notes, you're halfway home.

WRITING RAPIDLY

Most experienced writers find that the first draft should be written rapidly. Don't put down a sentence or two, stop, edit, and then start up again. If you become aware of writing badly, don't let this stop you, but move ahead to the next idea. Keep pushing on to the end of your writing session. If you planned to write for 30 minutes, keep writing the entire 30 minutes no matter how flat or flawed the writing seems to you. At the end of your session, take a break of 5 or 10 minutes and then return for a second session.

It's best not to lift your hands from the keyboard or from the paper during the drafting session you've set for yourself. Even if you run out of ideas, keep writing, since new ideas may pop into your head as you write. Write nonsense if you must, but keep writing. Refer frequently to your outline and quotations as you write; they will often inspire you to continue. When ideas and words cease to flow, look back at your thesis. If you can think of nothing else to say, repeat the thesis in different words and try to find a fresh example to illustrate it.

Look on a rough draft as an in-class writing assignment in which you forge ahead despite obstacles, with the added freedom that you need not submit it. It will be judged by no one but you.

Returning to the First Draft

After you have finished writing your draft, take a short break, come back to it, and see what is missing. Return to your notes and the text. Was there something you had planned to say that you failed to cover? Can you find lapses in your thinking? Omissions in your argument? Plan to spend another 20 or 30 minutes on fleshing out the first bare-bones rough draft.

Preliminary Editing

When you have finished with the first draft, it is time to prepare for a second by doing some provisional editing. The final, masterful editing comes later, after the final draft, when you polish your writing and ready it for the eyes of your readers. Now you need to ask questions chiefly about your main ideas and the development of your thinking.

Can you find in this first draft a direction, a strong central idea, a thesis? Is it the thesis you set out to argue in the first place? Now is the time to tinker with your thesis, to see if it works. If you discover that you were really going off in another direction, then try the new direction as perhaps the more interesting and valuable thesis.

What else is worthwhile in the hodgepodge of words? Are there sentences that stand out as significant? Passages that seem more alert and better expressed? Can you see ways to build more of your paper around these valuable sentences and passages?

What about organization? Unless you have followed an outline, it is unlikely that in this first rushed draft you have touched on your ideas and insights in the best order. If you drew up an outline previously, did you follow it in your draft?

Outlining from a Rough Draft

If you failed to outline before you began, can you now see ways to outline your material? Or perhaps you drew up an outline only to ignore it when you became caught up in writing the draft. Go through your rough draft paragraph by paragraph, noting the chief point in each. If you are using a computer, use boldface for the phrases, sentences, or passages that state the main idea of the paragraph. With pen and paper, underline these important elements. Then use them as the steps in your outline. Outlines based on a first draft can be effective for organizing your material for a second draft. Such outlines help you to see ways to rearrange your material. Ask yourself: What should come first? What should form the body of the paper? What is the best sequence of paragraphs to create the most coherent argument? Is there material at the end that really belongs early in the paper? Is there material that is in the wrong place that needs to be cut and moved? Is there material that should be cut and discarded?

FIRST DRAFTS ON THE COMPUTER

Keeping Your Fingers Moving on the Keyboard

As you work on your first draft, keep at the writing no matter how tempting you find other computer activities. Do not look up the date, or fool around with the puzzles, or review your files. This is not the time to pull out your past work for editing. When you're writing, write; don't cut and paste or run a spell check. These are editing procedures; their time comes later.

Printing Out Your Drafts

If you've written your first draft on a computer, print out your draft. You will want to do some editing right on the page where you can see larger chunks of your work and get a sense of the whole paper. After editing on the page for 15 or 20 minutes, go back to the screen and enter the editing into your document. As you enter the changes from the printed page, other editorial changes will come to mind.

Saving Frequently

Remember to save your writing and editing frequently. It is very discouraging to put in an hour or two of writing and editing only to lose everything through a system error or power failure. Print out your work at the end of a writing and editing session. Not only are printed pages (called *hard copy* in computer jargon) valuable to work on, they are an additional insurance in case you lose the disk with your files, or in case the disk fails to work. For these reasons most writers make back-up files of their work.

THE SECOND DRAFT

Once you are satisfied that you see how to build on the first draft to express and organize your basic ideas, launch into a second draft. A second draft, like the first, may be written rapidly, although many writers work more slowly and deliberately at this stage. Typically a second draft is built on the materials of the first. For example, you may decide to use three or four sentences from your first paragraph as the basis for a second draft of the beginning of your essay. If you are at a computer, copy the sentences and start writing with these sentences on the screen.

As you work on your second draft, keep turning to your first draft for passages to save in their entirety or in part, or for passages that contain important ideas that you want to reword. Even if your first draft seems awkward and poorly written, its content may be valuable, and here or there a sentence or phrase may be worth incorporating into your new draft.

The second draft should flow more easily than the first, and possibly you will be impressed with it as fluent and articulate enough to serve as the final draft. If you are still dissatisfied with your thinking, however, try another draft, or at least another draft of the paragraphs that don't work.

DIVIDING YOUR ROUGH DRAFT INTO SECTIONS

Just as you may find it helpful to divide your writing time into short sessions, you may want to work on your first draft bit by bit. Let us say that you plan to make three major points in your paper. You might use these as divisions to create three chunks of work during three drafting sessions. Such was the procedure used by the author of the following first draft of a paper on Shakespeare's *Romeo and Juliet.* The student used a computer for the rough drafts and planned three sessions of about 20 minutes each. Here is what the computer screen looked like as the student prepared for the drafting sessions:

STUDENT COMPUTER PLANNING

Thesis: Romeo's impetuousness causes him to rush into disastrous actions and brings about his death.

I.   Romeo's quick falling in love with Juliet.

> Juliet: Although I joy in thee,
> I have no joy of this contract to-night.
> It is too rash, too unadvised, too sudden;
> Too like the lightning, which doth cease to be

Ere one can say 'It lightens.' (2.2.116–120)

II. The friar's warnings and advice to go slowly.

Romeo: O, let us hence! I stand on sudden haste.
Friar: Wisely and slow. They stumble that run fast. (2.3.93–94)

Friar: These violent delights have violent ends
And in their triumph die, like fire and powder,
Which as they kiss, consume. . . .
Therefore love moderately: long love doth so;
Too swift arrives as tardy as too slow. (2.4.9–11; 14–15)

III. Romeo's haste in deciding to take his own life.

Romeo to apothecary as he buys poison:
Let me have
A dram of poison, such soon-speeding gear
As will disperse itself through all the veins
That the life-weary taker may fall dead,
And that the trunk may be discharged of breath
As violently as hasty powder fired
Doth hurry from the fatal cannon's womb. (5.1.59–65)

Notice that each step in the development of the paper will be built around quotations. The organization of the paper is simple and straightforward, following the chronology of the play. This makes it easy to combine into a single draft the three chunks of material produced during the three sessions. For each drafting session the student highlighted in bold the point to be argued and the quotations and placed them at the top of the screen. She used them as inspiration and guide for her drafting sessions. Here are the results of the drafting sessions before the student edited them:

STUDENT DRAFTING SESSION 1

I. Romeo's quick falling in love with Juliet.

Juliet: Although I joy in thee,
I have no joy of this contract to-night.
It is too rash, too unadvised, too sudden;
Too like the lightning, which doth cease to be
Ere one can say 'It lightens.' (2.2.116–120)

When the play begins Romeo is in love with Rosaline. He claims to love her deeply. Even his friends (which ones? Benvolio?) tell him to forget Rosaline, but he says he can't, he loves her too deeply. When they tell Romeo to go to the party with them at the Capulets he says no way why bother since he loves only Rosaline. But then as soon as he sees Juliet at the party he falls instantly in love with her. He totally forgets Rosaline. This shows how impetuous he is in his emotions. His emotions run away with him. He has no control of his emotions, and when they say love he doesn't even stop to consider what's happening.

He falls in love in an instant and then in the next moment he and Juliet are planning to marry. Juliet realizes the whole thing is way too hasty and she's worried about how fast they're moving.

Insert quote from Juliet.

These lines show her understanding of Romeo—good character analysis. You wonder why she goes along with his plans since she sees the danger. Anyway, not only do they get engaged that night, they plan to marry right away—no waiting. Their headlong rush into marriage shows the problem of their youthful, rash temperaments.

STUDENT DRAFTING SESSION 2

II. The friar's warnings and advice to go slowly.

> **Romeo: O, let us hence! I stand on sudden haste.**
> **Friar: Wisely and slow. They stumble that run fast. (2.3.93–94)**

> **Friar: These violent delights have violent ends**
> **And in their triumph die, like fire and powder,**
> **Which as they kiss, consume. . . .**
> **Therefore love moderately: long love doth so;**
> **Too swift arrives as tardy as too slow. (2.4.9–11; 14–15)**

When Romeo comes to the friar, the friar can't believe it. Here's Romeo in love with someone new. Just yesterday Romeo loved Rosaline, now he loves Juliet.

Insert the exchange between Romeo and friar.

The friar's second speech to Romeo adds to Juliet's image of lightning.

Insert friar's speech.

He talks about gunpowder and explosives, and points out the danger of violence. Romeo's love affair is violent, and his emotions are violent. He can't talk of anything but Juliet or think of anything else. He persuades the friar to marry the two of them, even though the friar sees the danger in their violent emotions. Romeo is very persuasive, so his impetuousness is catching.

The friar has the wisdom of maturity. Romeo contrasts with him as the impetuousness of youth. The play shows several contrasts of youth and age like this, for example the nurse and Juliet, showing how it's a major theme. The speed of the play—it moves rapidly just like Romeo. So the play as well has an impetuous quality to it, as if Shakespeare wrote the way Romeo loves, rushing from one event to the next.

STUDENT DRAFTING SESSION 3

III. Romeo's haste in deciding to take his own life.

Romeo to apothecary as he buys poison:
> **Let me have**
> **A dram of poison, such soon-speeding gear**
> **As will disperse itself through all the veins**
> **That the life-weary taker may fall dead,**
> **And that the trunk may be discharged of breath**
> **As violently as hasty powder fired**
> **Doth hurry from the fatal cannon's womb. (5.1.59–65)**

When Romeo learns from Balthasar that Juliet is dead, he goes to pieces. His violent haste takes over. He rushes to buy poison without stopping for a minute to think things through.

Insert speech to apothecary.

Here Romeo uses many words of speed, like the hasty powder. The hasty powder can remind us of the gunpowder imagery the friar used. Also he uses the word violently. The theme of violence from haste runs throughout the entire play.

Romeo is in such a big rush to kill himself. If Romeo had only waited, just waited a day or two, things would have worked out according to the friar's plan. Even if he waited just another hour, or a half hour, because Juliet wakes up from the sleeping potion just minutes after Romeo dies. This shows how the impetuousness is fatal—a couple of minutes make the difference between the plan working and the plan backfiring so both end up dead.

Romeo becomes desperate and foolish whenever he meets up with any opposition. His words to Balthasar at the graveyard show his haste and violence as well. He seems to be in a rush to die or to kill others. It's a tragedy of impatience.

Earlier Romeo had tried to kill himself with a knife when he was with the friar and the nurse, showing that his desperate haste is kind of a permanent part of his character, something he isn't aware of. The friar talked him out of it then. But nothing the friar says has any permanent influence on Romeo.

By dividing up the work into three blocks, the student felt more in control, less threatened by the size of the task. Since the student had these three documents from his drafting sessions in his computer, it was an easy matter for him to combine them. He did some minimal editing as he wrote, such as changing the more far-fetched misspellings and completing some fragments, but the results above include no editing of organization or content and obviously no polishing of the wording. In other words, it's a beginning, but a rough one; it needs considerable work before it is ready to submit. It has repetitions, illogical sequences, and rough transitions. With some preliminary editing, and after combining the text from the three drafting sessions, the paper took the following form:

STUDENT ROUGH DRAFT

Romeo's Impetuousness

At the beginning of Shakespeare's *Romeo and Juliet*, Romeo is in love with Rosaline. He claims to love her deeply and thinks of nothing else. But then as soon as he sees Juliet at the Capulets' party, he falls instantly in love with her. He never again mentions Rosaline and seems to forget her completely. This shows how impetuous he is in his emotions. He lets his emotions run away with him. This impetuousness is his character flaw and leads to his death.

The same night that he meets Juliet and falls in love with her he wants to marry her. In the balcony scene in the second act, he and Juliet plan their marriage, even though they have known each other for only a few hours. This haste reinforces the image of Romeo as emotionally uncontrolled that was introduced in the first act. Juliet realizes their plans are hasty and says to Romeo:

> Although I joy in thee,
> I have no joy of this contract to-night.
> It is too rash, too unadvised, too sudden;
> Too like the lightning, which doth cease to be
> Ere one can say 'It lightens.' (2.2.116–120)

These lines express her understanding of Romeo. She sees that his plans are "too rash," though she is willing to go along with them. The speech hints at the danger that waits for the two of them if they proceed with their plans in this "unadvised" way.

When Romeo comes to the friar, the friar is amazed at the quick change in Romeo's emotions. Yesterday he was in love with Rosaline, today with Juliet. He tries to caution Romeo about going ahead too quickly and carelessly. When Romeo says to the friar, "O, let us hence! I stand on sudden haste," the friar answers, "Wisely and slow. They stumble that run fast" (2.3.93–94). The word "stumble" adds to the idea of danger waiting for Romeo if he rushes ahead with his plans to marry Juliet. The friar makes his warning to Romeo explicit in these lines:

> These violent delights have violent ends
> And in their triumph die, like fire and powder,
> Which as they kiss, consume. . . .
> Therefore love moderately: long love doth so;
> Too swift arrives as tardy as too slow. (2.4.9–11; 14–15)

The friar's speech points out the violence in Romeo's impetuousness. His talk about gunpowder and explosives underlines the dangers Romeo is running by behaving with so little emotional control. These lines help to define the friar as someone with the wisdom of maturity. He is a direct contrast with Romeo's youthful impetuousness.

Many of Romeo's actions throughout the play show his dangerous tendency to rush into action. His killing Tybalt is a good example. Then when Romeo finds out that he is banished for this murder he instantly threatens to kill himself. He is prevented from taking his own life by the friar, but the attempt shows how his impetuousness is dangerous to himself and brings in the theme of suicide.

Romeo's suicidal violence is instantly aroused when he hears from Balthasar that Juliet is dead. His violent haste takes over, and he rushes to buy poison without stopping to think. His words to the apothecary as he buys the poison express his violence and haste:

> Let me have
> A dram of poison, such soon-speeding gear
> As will disperse itself through all the veins
> That the life-weary taker may fall dead,
> And that the trunk may be discharged of breath
> As violently as hasty powder fired
> Doth hurry from the fatal cannon's womb. (5.1.59–65)

Romeo then rushes to Juliet's tomb to kill himself. His violent haste ruins the plan that the friar has worked out. If Romeo had only waited another 15 or 20 minutes before swallowing the poison, he could have been reunited with Juliet and the action of the play would have ended happily. Just a few minutes after Romeo succumbs to the poison Juliet awakens. This close miss underlines the idea of the danger of Romeo's impetuousness and shows that *Romeo and Juliet* is a tragedy of youthful haste.

If you compare this second draft with the material generated in the first three drafting sessions, you will see that the student has cut away a considerable amount of material. Her first drafting sessions produced more than enough in the way of commentary and ideas, and she enjoyed the luxury of having material to spare. Notice that she moved the final paragraph from drafting session 3 to an earlier position in her essay since it refers to an action earlier in the play. Thus she kept to her organizational plan of using the play's chronology as the basis for her writing sequence.

The student worked on this material on a computer, making much of the change from the three initial drafting sessions to the second complete draft a fairly simple matter of cutting and pasting. She also changed many of the sentences and word choices. But notice that the content did not change in any fundamental way, although some ideas that are not central to the topic, such as the ideas in the final paragraph of the second drafting session, were cut. Thus the topic has been more clearly focused. The thesis—that Romeo's impetuousness is his character flaw and leads to his death—is stated more clearly and forcefully in the second draft.

The student found that the second draft took about 45 minutes to an hour to complete. She was happy with the results, and decided that with only a little more proofreading and polishing she would submit it as the final draft.

8

BEGINNINGS & ENDINGS

- **The Opening Paragraph**
- **Identifying the Texts under Discussion**
- **Introducing Your Thesis**
- **False Starts**
- **Sample Beginnings**
- **Conclusions**
- **False Endings**

THE OPENING PARAGRAPH

Writing an opening paragraph might be compared to dealing with Medusa: It can paralyze you. "This had better be good," you say, struggling with the perfect phrasing to open your paper. If you insist on perfection from the beginning, you may fall victim to the paralysis called "writer's block."

Medusa is best handled indirectly, and the same is true of first paragraphs to literary papers. You avoid paralysis by beginning the process of writing with whatever comes first to mind, rather than with what you believe should come first in the essay. In other words, separate the process of writing from the organization of your paper. The process of writing often moves along better if you forget the opening paragraph until you have written your thesis, assembled your quotations, tried some of the prewriting techniques of Chapter 1, and written one or two drafts of your paper.

Of course you need to start your first draft with a beginning, a way into the topic, but don't feel it must be the paragraph which will serve for the opener in your final draft. After you've finished the drafts, look through your material to see what might serve as an opening paragraph. Naturally you'll need to work on the paragraph to make it effective as an opening.

IDENTIFYING THE TEXTS UNDER DISCUSSION

Providing the Author's Name and the Title of the Work

Your opening paragraph should identify the author (or authors) and the title of the work you are setting out to discuss. Consider the problems posed by the following first paragraph:

STUDENT INTRODUCTORY PARAGRAPH

Most readers find Mr. Rochester an attractive and sympathetic figure whose first marriage has ended tragically through no fault of his own. He is seen as highly emotional but basically kind and just toward Bertha Mason. The woman's insanity is considered to be her own fault. Through her moral failings she has aggravated an inherited family weakness. But this view of Mr. Rochester whitewashes his character and makes him too innocent. In fact, he must share the blame for Bertha Mason's madness. He is part of her emotional problems.

Some readers may know by the names that this introductory paragraph concerns characters in Charlotte Brontë's *Jane Eyre*, but by no means will everyone know this. It is an obligation in writing literary discussion to indicate what literature is being discussed, even if you feel you are writing primarily to fulfill an assignment in which your readers—your teacher and classmates— know the work you are discussing. Here is a revision of the first sentence in the above paragraph that includes the vital information:

Most readers of Charlotte Brontë's *Jane Eyre* find Mr. Rochester an attractive and sympathetic figure whose first marriage has ended tragically through no fault of his own.

INTRODUCING YOUR THESIS

Awaking Interest with a Forceful Thesis

Opening paragraphs should awaken the reader's interest. In a literary paper this awakening of interest often depends on a lively and forceful thesis that brings into focus the argument of the paper. The most direct approach is to state your thesis in the first paragraph.

Examine again the paragraph above concerning Mr. Rochester in Brontë's *Jane Eyre*. The paragraph concludes with a clear assertion. The thesis to be developed and supported is stated forcefully in the two last sentences. There is no doubt where the author stands on the question. The writer has sharpened the impact of the thesis by first stating the conventional view that his thesis contradicts. The argument has begun, and if you know the novel and care about the characters, you will probably be interested in how the author will develop and support his assertion.

Stating Your Thesis Early

There are many advantages to stating your thesis in the opening paragraph. Often you want to state it in the first sentence. Examine the following paragraphs to see how each takes a direct approach to the topic:

STUDENT INTRODUCTORY PARAGRAPHS

In "The Fall of the House of Usher," Edgar Allan Poe embarks on a journey into the darkness of the human mind. Poe's main point, evoked most strongly in the story through the image of the reawakening of the buried Madeline, is that whatever the rational conscious mind attempts to suppress, the irrational subconscious mind will reveal.

An Enemy of the People can be seen as Henrik Ibsen's statement about the lonely champions of truth. "The strongest man in the world is the man who stands alone," Dr. Stockmann, the hero of the play, says in words that express the author's conviction. The mass of common people, the majority, are mistaken. Truth can be found only in the individual with the courage to be independent.

In *Great Expectations*, Charles Dickens expresses his dislike of the upper classes and the rich. He makes it clear that his favorites are people like Joe Gargery and Biddy, humble people with no social pretensions and no ambitions to live among the rich and the mighty. These simple, good people are contrasted with snobs like Bentley Drummle, who represents what Dickens hated most about the upper classes.

Each of these opening paragraphs provides the name of the author, the title of the literary work, and a succinct statement of the thesis. Each moves rapidly to discuss specifics of the literature and names at least one character as an illustration of the thesis.

Your Paper's Title & Introductory Paragraph

Your introductory paragraph might pick up and develop an idea or image in your title. It should not, however, merely repeat the topic of the title. For example, if your title is "Hamlet's Melancholy," begin with more than just a sentence that says, "Hamlet had a melancholy disposition," which paraphrases the title. Instead, try at once to indicate what you plan to say about the topic (e.g, "Hamlet's melancholy causes his indecision in taking revenge").

Consider, for example, the following title and opening paragraph:

STUDENT INTRODUCTORY PARAGRAPH

The Questionable Ghost

Shakespeare's *Hamlet* opens with a question. "Who's there?" are the first words spoken in the darkness surrounding the castle at Elsinore. The question echoes throughout the play and is especially relevant to the ghost. Who is this ghost who appears in the first act? Are his intentions good or evil? Has he come to tempt the young prince to do evil or to encourage him to perform an honorable act? Does Hamlet risk his sanity by going off with the ghost and listening to him sympathetically? These questions are part of the basic question of "Who's there?" and give the first act and the entire play a mood of doubt and uncertainty. Hamlet calls the ghost "questionable," and the questions that the ghost raises are never fully answered. The ghost is questionable to the very end.

This opening paragraph contains a number of virtues worth examining. It moves at once to a direct engagement with the literary work. It quotes the play and refers to the setting, thus drawing readers to consider not only the thesis of the paper—that the ghost is questionable or uncertain—but the play itself. Consider how much less successful the second sentence would be if the author had written, " 'Who's there?' are the first words spoken in the play." The reference to the darkness surrounding the castle at Elsinore conjures up an image from the play. It is part of the author *showing* rather than just *telling*, and it encourages the readers to visualize the scene as well as understand the argument. Thus in the opening paragraph the writer moves quickly to fulfill one of the goals of good literary discussion, which is a close scrutiny of the work under question.

This opening also begins the paper with the beginning of the literary work under discussion, a logical starting place that suggests the paper will proceed in an orderly fashion. It relates the paper's thesis to the paper's title and begins the development of the thesis, so that readers can sense not only what main point is being asserted, but also something about how the point is to be supported and developed. Finally, the paragraph uses a number of questions, a fitting technique in a paper examining a questionable character and attempting to demonstrate that questions remain unanswered at the end of the literary work.

FALSE STARTS

Avoiding Discussion of Your Paper

Open your paper with a statement about the literary work, not about your own paper. The following introduction includes a worthwhile thesis, but the focus of the statement is on the paper, not the literary work: "In the following pages I shall attempt to prove that Hamlet's indecisiveness is due to his melancholy over his mother's remarriage." This could be revised as follows: "In Shakespeare's *Hamlet*, the young prince is indecisive because of his melancholy over his mother's remarriage."

Avoiding Broad Generalizations

Students are often attracted to broad generalizations that seem to sweep up a large amount of literary material into a single sentence. They may feel that such generalizations provide a valuable way to move from the general to the specific. Sometimes generalizations do this (this paragraph, for example, moves from a generalization to a specific example), but often they remain too vague and general to provide a forceful opening. Here, for example, are the opening sentences from an essay on Mark Twain's *The Adventures of Huckleberry Finn*:

STUDENT INTRODUCTORY PARAGRAPH

The early-childhood environment that surrounds a person growing up tends to be a major factor in determining the person's opinions and prejudices. If someone grows up in an environment of racism, he or she will probably become a racist. In the American South during the days of Mark Twain, children commonly grew up in a racist environment, so they became racists themselves. Huck Finn finally avoids being a racist after some of his experiences with Jim, but when he first grows up he expresses the racism of the white society around him and especially of Pap.

Huck's change from racist to someone who cares for Jim is a major theme of the novel. . . .

The all-purpose generalizations about environmental influences and character formation are distractions from the thesis of the paper concerning Huck's changes. The generalizations do not arise from the literature but seem to have escaped from a paper in the social sciences, an impression reinforced by the social-sciences jargon ("early-childhood environment" as a "major factor").

There are effective introductory paragraphs that begin with generalizations and move to the literature as a specific illustration, but in contrast to the paragraph above, their effectiveness depends on the direct relevance of the generalizations to the literary work under discussion. The paragraph above on Huckleberry Finn was rewritten as follows so that its use of generalization does not lead away from the literature but into it:

REVISED STUDENT INTRODUCTORY PARAGRAPH

Huck Finn grew up in a racist town where slavery was the rule and where the whites assumed as a matter of course that blacks are inferior. It is not surprising, therefore, that Huck begins his life with racist views. He learns this racism from the white adults in his town, and especially from his father, who often expresses a very demeaning view of blacks. But Huck changes his views as he leaves his town and travels the Mississippi with Jim, the runaway slave, showing that the negative influences of early childhood can be escaped. Huck's change in attitude toward Jim and his increasing respect for him as he comes to know the black man better are major themes of Mark Twain's *The Adventures of Huckleberry Finn.*

Notice that the generalizations in this revised paragraph concern the people in the novel, not people in general. Thus the general statements arise from a study of the novel and apply to the theme of the novel.

Avoiding Historical Generalizations

Students are sometimes tempted to write as if the purpose of their paper were to offer awards for historical achievements, speaking in their opening paragraphs of Shakespeare as "the greatest playwright in English," Robert Frost as "America's finest nature poet," Ernest Hemingway as "America's foremost author of war novels." Such assertions cannot be proved, and they annoy readers and cause them to question on what authority the author makes such judgments. In any case, historical generalizations belong in a paper on historical topics. If you write such a paper you had better be an authority on the topic in which you offer sweeping historical generalizations. If you want to call Frost America's finest nature poet, you must read all of Frost and all of the other American nature poets; otherwise you are either repeating what you have read or heard somewhere or offering unsubstantiated bluster.

The following opening paragraph begins with weak historical generalizations that can be neither proved nor disproved. Notice that the generalizations lead nowhere. The author tosses out the idea of greatness but has no intentions of discussing the topic. The same holds true for the statement about books "read by millions." Such a statement might lead into an essay on popular taste in Dickens' day or on the popularity of Dickens' novels, but these are not topics the student means to discuss. What the student does mean to discuss is introduced in sentences three and four, and these could with some rewriting become workable introductory statements.

STUDENT INTRODUCTORY PARAGRAPH

Charles Dickens is one of the greatest novelists of all time, and his books have been read by millions of readers. His novels are interesting and informative and show us a lot about the times when he lived. In *Great Expectations*, for example, he showed us how people lived in a small village and in the big city of London. He made these contrasting places very real and brought them alive for the reader.

When the student author of the paragraph on Dickens recognized that her opening lacked a clear focus and a thesis, she revised it to focus on the contrast of village life and city life as follows. Her opening is noteworthy for including specific details of Pip's life in London to support her generalization about life in London being "elegant, complicated, and expensive."

REVISED STUDENT INTRODUCTORY PARAGRAPH

Dickens' *Great Expectations* includes contrasting pictures of life in a small village and life in London. The novel opens by showing Pip's life in a simple country village near the Thames River. Pip lives with with his sister and her husband, Joe Gargery, a blacksmith, and the picture of Joe Gargery helps to establish Dickens' view of village life as simple and ordinary. By contrast life in London is elegant, complicated, and expensive, as we see when Pip moves to Barnard's Inn and quickly runs into debt buying furniture and clothing, joining a club called the Finches of the Grove, and employing a "boy in boots" to serve as his butler.

Avoiding Random Judgments

The following opening paragraph on Shakespeare's *Romeo and Juliet* offers a grab bag of pointless comments. To state that the play is tragic and has caused readers to cry is to offer commonplaces, not criticism. Don't state the obvious; instead, use your papers as a chance to explore your reactions and insights into literature.

STUDENT INTRODUCTORY PARAGRAPH

Shakespeare's *Romeo and Juliet* has always been admired as a great love story. It is filled with excellent love poetry as well as intriguing characters. It is a very tragic story and has made generations of readers cry over its unhappy ending.

SAMPLE BEGINNINGS

Notice in the following examples of successful opening sentences and paragraphs that the author has moved quickly to a direct consideration of the literary work. Most false beginnings move away from the literature. As you begin your paper, keep in mind that you want to engage in direct commentary on the characters, action, setting, plot, language, theme, or some other aspect of the literary work you are setting out to discuss. Notice how the following beginnings all take as their point of departure something specific in the literature:

Beginning with a Direct Quotation

Samuel Taylor Coleridge begins his poem "Kubla Khan" with the lines, "In Xanadu did Kubla Khan / A stately pleasure-dome decree," immediately pulling his readers into an exotic, foreign world composed of caves of ice, a deep chasm, meandering streams, and sunny dome of pleasure.

Beginning with a Character

Willy Loman suffers from a failure of confidence. As the hero of Arthur Miller's *The Death of a Salesman*, he infects his family and the entire atmosphere of the play with his sense of failure. He fears he can do nothing right; he especially fears that he can no longer provide for his family because he can no longer be an effective salesman.

Beginning with a Scene or an Episode

Shakespeare opens Act 5 of *Hamlet* with the grave diggers, two men described as clowns whose words and actions create comic relief in the midst of the tragedy.

Beginning with the Theme

Graham Greene's "The Destructors" provides several examples of his theme that humans are senselessly destructive. This theme is illustrated by the foreground actions of the boys in the gang who destroy for no clear reasons a house designed by Christopher Wren and by the background actions of adults who waged World War II and destroyed much of London.

CONCLUSIONS

Ending with Your Thesis

A strong conclusion leaves the reader with the feeling that the writer has concluded his or her argument and proved his or her point. A concluding paragraph should return to the thesis.

The most difficult papers to conclude are those without a thesis. Just as a strong argument helps you to set out with firm steps, so too it enables you to come to a clear finish. If you find that you are having trouble finishing your paper, look again at your thesis. Is it truly an argument? If your paper offers instead a series of random observations or plot summary, at the end it will likely trail off rather than reach a conclusion.

Examine the following two paragraphs, the introduction and the conclusion to a paper on *Hamlet* (the introductory paragraph was included in the discussion of introductory paragraphs), to see how the final paragraph returns to the thesis and brings the argument to a close:

STUDENT INTRODUCTORY PARAGRAPH

The Questionable Ghost

Shakespeare's *Hamlet* opens with a question. "Who's there?" are the first words spoken in the darkness surrounding the castle at Elsinore. The question echoes throughout the play and is especially relevant to the ghost. Who is this ghost who appears in the first act? Are his intentions good or evil? Has he come to tempt the young prince to do evil or to encourage him to perform an honorable act? Does Hamlet risk his sanity by going off with the ghost and listening to him sympathetically? These questions are part of the basic question of "Who's there?" and give the first act and the entire play a mood of doubt and uncertainty. Hamlet calls the ghost "questionable," and the questions that the ghost raises are never fully answered. The ghost is questionable to the very end.

STUDENT CONCLUDING PARAGRAPH

The play ends with some things clear and definite: Hamlet has killed Claudius and ended his corrupt and false rule. The prince has taken steps to rid Denmark of evil, but it is by no means clear that a better government will succeed Claudius. Hamlet is dead, and the uncertainty of evil hangs over the court. Nothing in the play has settled the truth about the ghost, and so to the end the play continues in the doubting spirit that was expressed in the opening question, "Who's there?" When the final curtain falls, there is still no answer to this question.

Note that the conclusion above does not restate the original thesis in the same words; it returns to the thesis, applying it to the action of the play in specific ways, thus adding to the reader's understanding of the thesis at the same time it brings the argument to a close.

The concluding paragraph that follows on Sophocles' *Oedipus Rex* and the modern film *The Official Story* works well because it offers a summary statement—that humanity will always struggle but has the power to succeed—and focuses on the conclusion of the play:

STUDENT CONCLUDING PARAGRAPH

Throughout history, people have asked themselves who they are and where they come from. Both *Oedipus Rex* and *The Official Story*, although written over two thousand years apart, portray two characters struggling to answer these questions about themselves. The search for the truth is all-consuming, but it is a necessary one if humanity is to live peacefully. The choragos ends the play with a passage which applies to all humanity:

> Let every man in mankind's frailty
> Consider his last day; and let none
> Presume on his good fortune until he finds
> Life, at his death, a memory without pain.

The quotation from *Oedipus Rex* adds to the success of this conclusion, especially because the words apply to the end of life. Thus several concluding images combine here—the end of human life, the end of the play, the end of the paper—to create a strong sense of finality.

FALSE ENDINGS

Avoiding Discussion of Your Paper

Just as you do not want to begin a paper with words about your own writing, you also want to avoid a similar focus at the end: "Thus this paper has demonstrated that Lady Macbeth was the instigator of the evil that brought Macbeth to power and ultimately ruined his life and her own."

Avoiding Repetition of Your Conclusions

If you have made your conclusions clear in the body of your paper, you probably do not need to summarize or repeat them in a final paragraph. Long thesis papers that have taken readers through complex arguments and offered considerable information sometimes gain clarity and conclusiveness at the end by repeating the main points, but papers of five or six pages rarely need this kind of reiteration. However, your instructor may be following the five-paragraph essay model, which dictates a concluding paragraph wherein the three major points of the essay are restated. To many readers, such restatement seems forced and mechanical, the fulfillment of a formula rather than a natural conclusion, but your instructor may wish you to use such an ending because of its value in teaching you how to bring an argument to a close. If you have been assigned to write according to the five-paragraph model, search for fresh ways to conclude your paper. Avoid using in the final paragraph the words and phrases that you used in developing your argument.

Avoiding Judgments of Approval or Disapproval

You cannot write a forceful paper from vague judgments such as, "Shakespeare was a great writer," and endings should avoid similar judgments: "Lady Macbeth shows Shakespeare's greatness in creating characters and illustrates why he was the foremost dramatist of his time and perhaps of all time."

Avoiding a Focus on Your Reactions

Don't shift the focus of your paper from an interpretation to your reactions: "I found Mark Twain's novel a fascinating work because I could relate so easily to Huck Finn." At the end of your paper, you want your readers to be thinking about the literary work, not your feelings about it.

Avoiding the Introduction of a New Topic

Your concluding paragraph is not the place to introduce a new topic. If a topic interests you and is related to your thesis, then introduce it and discuss it in the body of the paper, not at the end.

9

SOME QUESTIONS OF STYLE

- Standard Formal English
- Clarity
- Emphasis
- Avoiding Sweeping Generalizations
- Economy & Simplicity
- Freshness
- Special Problems of Literary Papers

STANDARD FORMAL ENGLISH

Using Standard English

Standard English is the language of textbooks, newspapers, and most magazines. In other words, it is the language of the printed page. Except for rare formal occasions, it is not the language of speech. Most speech can be labelled *colloquial*; it makes use of informal expressions, fragments, and slang in ways inappropriate for formal written English. Novels, plays, poems, and other works of imaginative writing often purposefully use colloquial language, and you may use it in letters, journals, and other informal writing. But when you come to writing papers for your academic courses, you must use formal English (unless your instructor tells you otherwise).

Because you do not speak formal English, you use it less often than the colloquial language, and consequently you may find it poses more of a struggle to write. For example, in a class discussion you might say, "At the end of the play Oedipus kind of goes crazy and jabs out his eyes." You probably do not need to be told you should not write such a sentence in a formal character analysis of Oedipus. Instinctively you sense that the language of written academic discussion demands a precision and formality not expected in common speech.

Among other differences distinguishing it from the common colloquial language, standard formal English avoids contractions. Instead of writing, "Oedipus can't figure out what his problem is," you would write, "Oedipus cannot determine the cause of his problem." You should avoid as well the colloquial use of words and phrases such as *got* or *a lot of* (e.g., "Oedipus has got a lot of problems"). This means that writing a literary paper requires an effort to be correct that you do not experience when speaking or writing informally. You may feel that colloquial speech comes naturally, whereas formal written English must be learned.

Avoiding an Overly Elevated Style

Although you should avoid colloquial diction in a literary paper, you should also avoid ornate, overly elevated language. Don't try to impress your readers with an erudite vocabulary and complex sentences, such as the following:

 When Hamlet's idealizations of his now-deceased father are brought into juxtaposition with his mother's indifference to the disparity between her present and her previous husband, an inevitable antagonism arises.

Not only does such a sentence grate on the ears, but it also perplexes the mind. Just what is being said here? Writers eager to show off a lofty vocabulary are especially tempted by abstract words such as we find in this sentence (e.g., "idealizations," "juxtaposition," "disparity"). Too many abstract words drain writing of energy. They make it vague and pompous.

Your writing should sound natural but dressed up enough to go out in public to an important occasion—neither tattered jeans nor white tie and tails. To gain naturalness, read your papers aloud. Read them to your friends, or have them read them back to you. These strategies help you to develop your ear for fluent style.

CLARITY

Clarity as the Primary Goal

Literary essays are a form of expository writing, writing that explains. First and foremost, explanations must be understandable. When you make them graceful and fluent as well, you deserve congratulations, but keep in mind that your primary aim is clarity. Keep asking yourself whether you are making your concepts and ideas understandable to others. Your classmates can help you with this. If you have the opportunity to work with your classmates in a peer editing session, ask them especially about the parts of your essay that express your thesis and develop your argument.

EMPHASIS

Writing Emphatically

Write with emphasis. You gain emphasis with the choice of the right word. Mark Twain tells us that the difference between the right word and the wrong word is like the difference between lightning and a lightning bug. The mistaken way to emphasis comes from expressions such as "very significant," "totally worthless," "extremely important," "really outstanding." These words are modifiers—adverbs and adjectives that as a class add less emphasis than do nouns and verbs. Words like *very, totally, extremely,* and *really* are intensifiers, modifiers that have no meaning in themselves, but are used to intensify the meaning of adjectives they modify. Frequently they do just the reverse. We all know how flat a joke is when the teller is forced to assure us repeatedly that it's "really, really funny." Just as you do not make something comic by such words, you do not make it significant by relying on intensifiers. Revise sentences that include adjectives and intensifiers:

> *Weak:* "Romeo's haste is very important in his downfall."
> *Revised for emphasis:* "Romeo's haste causes him to rush to his downfall."

Avoiding the Lame Passive

Inexperienced writers often rely too heavily on verbs in the passive voice (when the subject of the verb does not perform the action), such as the verb *was accomplished* in the following sentence: "Hamlet's revenge was accomplished only in the final act of the play." What is wrong with using verbs in the passive voice? Perhaps an example will make clear the weakness of the passive better than an explanation. Most of us know the story of George Washington and the cherry tree. Young George's confession in the passive reads as follows: "Father, I cannot tell a lie. A cherry tree was chopped down."

Such use of the verb earns the label *lame passive.* The word *lame* indicates the verb's weakness at conveying important information. Who cut down the tree? Politicians and bureaucrats often escape into the lame passive precisely because it obscures who is performing the action described by the verb: "Errors were committed," they say; "A mistake occurred." This probably does not make for good politics; it certainly makes for bad writing. It is both confusing and evasive.

To return to the sentence on Hamlet's revenge: The passive voice, *was accomplished*, suggests that possibly someone else accomplished the revenge for Hamlet. Is this what the author means? If not, the author makes the point clearer by the use of the active verb: "Hamlet accomplished his revenge in the final act of the play."

In certain academic disciplines, notably the sciences, the passive voice of verbs is preferred for some forms of writing, such as reports of laboratory experiments: "An increase in the release of oxygen was observed at temperatures above 90 degrees centigrade." In writing literary papers, there are times when the passive voice is preferable, as in this statement: "For years Dickens' novels were read as popular entertainment; today they are viewed as serious literature." The passive works better here because it allows *Dickens' novels* to serve as the subject. To recast the sentence for the active voice— "For years people read Dickens' novels as popular literature; today people read them as serious literature"—changes the meaning.

Inexperienced writers of literary papers fall into the passive voice without realizing it, and this inadvertent use often causes confusion. Avoiding the passive voice demands that you search out your inadvertent use of the passive and search for ways of clarifying your writing by making your verbs active.

The following passage of literary discussion presents some of the problems created by careless use of the passive:

At the beginning of *Oedipus Rex*, Oedipus is seen as an admirable leader. He is known as intelligent because he solves the riddle of the Sphinx. But at the end of the play he is regarded as just the opposite, as an evil man, a criminal.

This example shows how the passive creates confusion. Who sees Oedipus as "an admirable leader"? Sophocles? The people of Thebes? The audience watching the play? The author of the paper? Each of these possible interpretations provides a different way of viewing the statement. The next two sentences are equally confusing. Who knows him to be intelligent? Who comes to regard him as evil?

The student revised this passage as follows:

In the beginning of *Oedipus Rex*, the citizens of Thebes see Oedipus as an admirable leader. They believe him to be intelligent because he has solved the riddle of the Sphinx. But at the end of the play, the Thebans regard him as evil, a criminal.

Avoiding the Overuse of Linking Verbs

The linking verbs are forms of the verb *to be* or *to have* along with *seems, appears,* and *looks.* These verbs lack punch. They present no activity, just existence or appearance. Here is an example of their overuse with the linking verbs in bold:

Huck Finn **is** a realistic person, which we see when he wants to free Jim as quickly as possible. He **is** contrasted with Tom Sawyer, who **is** not as realistic. Tom **seems** more romantic and impractical. He **has** many far-fetched, impractical ideas for freeing Jim.

A revision using an active verb:

Huck Finn's realistic approach to freeing Jim **contrasts** with Tom Sawyer's more romantic, impractical and far-fetched ideas.

Using Strong Verbs

Strong verbs assert themselves. They alert the reader's attention, speak emphatically, and perform as verbs should—which means that they show action. You strengthen your verbs by putting them in the active voice and by avoiding overuse of the linking verbs. In the following discussion of Thomas Hardy's *Tess of the d'Urbervilles*, all the strong verbs (verbs that are not linking verbs and those not in the passive voice) have been highlighted in bold:

STUDENT PARAGRAPH

   Tess **accepts** the responsibility for the welfare of her family and **agrees to drive** the beehives to market, demonstrating early in her life a maturity and moral sense lacking in her parents. Her father **behaves** in his usual irresponsible way, drinking himself into a condition where he **cannot accomplish** his work. Tess **must take** his place. Thus she **begins** her journey into life, the one member of the family responsible and mature enough **to take** the beehives to market. The journey **ends** in a disaster with the death of their horse, but it would be foolish **to blame** Tess for this accident. She **has** not **behaved** carelessly; instead, some perversity of fate **has brought** about the accident. Readers **might expect** such an accident **to befall** the "slack-twisted" Jack Durbeyfield; it is a mark of Hardy's irony that it **occurs** to Tess.

AVOIDING SWEEPING GENERALIZATIONS

Many students feel that sweeping generalizations provide emphasis, and in their desire to be emphatic they will write passages such as the following:

Everybody in Huck Finn's hometown was a racist and hated the blacks. In Mark Twain's day none of the whites in the South would ever think of helping a slave escape, so Huck was doing something that everyone would condemn.

What is the problem with these sweeping generalizations? Quite simply, they are inaccurate. Sweeping generalizations usually are. One piece of contrary evidence destroys a sweeping generalization. The first sentence above is obviously false, for many of the people in Huck Finn's hometown were themselves black. Of course the student writing that "everybody was a racist and hated the blacks" was not thinking of the blacks in the town, but the word *everybody* nevertheless includes them. Furthermore, the student could not account even for the feelings of all white people in the town, because Mark Twain has not given us a complete survey of the attitudes of all the people of Huck's town. He has told us just a few things about very few people in the town. True, he has suggested that many of the whites had condescending, racist views of the blacks by having some of the whites express such views, but this is a different situation from what the author of the sweeping generalization has asserted. The above sweeping generalizations might be rewritten as follows:

Most of the whites in Huck Finn's hometown were racists who looked on the blacks as inferior. Few Southern whites in Mark Twain's day would help runaway slaves, and most would have condemned Huck for helping Jim.

These revisions show greater honesty and thoughtfulness. They also reflect the student's limitations in knowledge, for in fact the student at best has only a rough impression of how the people of Mark Twain's day felt about the topic of slaves or anything else. Sweeping generalizations should be used only by authorities with confident and thorough knowledge of the subject.

ECONOMY & SIMPLICITY

We are all familiar with the situation that occurs when a writer, to meet the demands of an assignment, pads his or her paper with extra words. Rather than writing, "By the end of the raft journey, Huck Finn has developed an admiration for Jim," the writer stuffs in extra phrases: "Thus it is easy to recognize that, by the end of the raft journey, with new insights into the character and values of his raft companion and an enlarged sense of Jim's essential worthiness as a human being, Huck now has a real admiration for the runaway slave." The first sentence contains 15 words, the second 48. What has been gained by this tripling of words? Nothing. What has been lost?

Clarity and precision, most obviously. With them goes economy of expression, an aspect of a vigorous style. The second sentence is pompous and ugly as well as unclear.

Avoid introducing your statements with phrases such as, "It is easy to recognize that" or "It is my opinion that." These phrases not only clutter the sentence with unnecessary words, but also force on a simple idea a complex sentence structure using a subordinate clause beginning "that." Be direct. Write, "Lady Macbeth is ambitious," not "It is obvious that Lady Macbeth is ambitious." Notice how economy of expression enhances clarity; write what you mean in a few strong words and you will usually write clearly.

There are many common wordy phrases that writers use without thinking. Notice how the following phrases can be reduced to a single word:

> *at this point in time, at the present time:* cut to *now*
> *due to the fact that:* cut to *because*
> *in the event of:* cut to *if*
> *in the majority of instances:* cut to *usually*

Wordy sentences are typically long; examine your prose for sentences that sprawl over several lines. Can you cut these monsters without cutting away ideas and information? If so, do it. Even if you don't cut many words away, by cutting the long sentences into shorter ones you will probably gain clarity.

Avoiding a Choppy Style

Avoid writing long, cumbersome sentences, but do not retreat into a false simplicity. A series of brief, simple sentences can make a passage choppy, as in the following sample:

Hawthorne did not look favorably on the Puritans. He thought their morality was too severe. He wrote *A Scarlet Letter* to show how severe and unforgiving they were. In it the Puritans are depicted as cruel.

Revised:

In writing *A Scarlet Letter*, Hawthorne expressed his critical view of the Puritans by showing them as morally severe, unforgiving, and cruel.

Keeping It Simple

Select words that are familiar and short. Shakespeare wrote his most famous soliloquy with words noteworthy for their simplicity: "To be or not to be." Short familiar words add power and precision to your writing. "Her face had a scar" is better than "Her countenance suffered from disfigurement." "Hamlet kills Polonius" works better than "Hamlet exterminates Polonius." Consider the loss of precision in the following: "Huck Finn involved himself in a lot of prevarication." Here is the same thought expressed more simply: "Huck Finn told many lies."

Prefer the simple, more common form of words; select *beauty* rather than *beauteousness, evil* rather than *evilness, discomfort* rather than *uncomfortableness*. The positive form of words packs more punch than the negative: *cruelty* is more forceful than *unkindness, hateful* better than *unlikable*. Notice that the positive word is typically shorter. Consider the following passage of negatives along with its revision to see how the first is evasive:

Hester Prynne is certainly not unattractive, and her daughter, Pearl, is also not lacking in some of the qualities people like in children, though of course she also has her not-so-good aspects.

Revised:

Hester Prynne is beautiful, and her daughter, Pearl, has many likeable qualities along with her mischievousness.

FRESHNESS

Fresh perceptions in fresh language—this is a goal of good writing. Like stale bread, stale language repels us. We are drawn to good writing because it conveys in fresh and lively ways the observations of someone who has looked at life and literature with fresh eyes. Not all of us can be brilliant original stylists, but we can all work to avoid relying on secondhand thoughts expressed in secondhand words. No matter how original our ideas and observations, if we express them in secondhand words they will seem flat, stale, and unoriginal.

Avoiding Jargon

Jargon is the special language of a trade, profession, or field of study. The jargon that invades literary papers often arises from the social sciences. It can produce sentences like the following:

Pearl does not interface with a peer group, since none of her peers will associate with her, and so she fails to learn the important interpersonal skills of the maturation process.

Revised:

Without friends her own age, Pearl does not learn how to behave with other children.

Avoid words and phrases like *interpersonal relationships, input, interface, the bottom line, on the down side.* They are jargon, and their common use gives them the stale quality of cliché.

Avoiding Clichés

A *cliché* is a stale phrase ("cute as a button") or statement ("you can't judge a book by its cover") used where a fresh one is needed. Instead of arousing interest, clichés bore the reader. Avoid sentences, phrases, and words that have become habits of speech, for they reveal that no imagination and little thought has been exercised in their use. Here is an example: "Thus at the end of *Great Expectations,* a sadder but wiser Pip reflects on his life and recognizes that behind every dark cloud there is a silver lining."

Typically, clichés are vague, as in the use of "relate" in the following sentence: "Bentley Drummle just can't relate to Pip and Herbert." Does this mean that Drummle doesn't talk to Pip and Herbert, or that he doesn't like them, or that he ignores them, or that when he does socialize with them he does so in a condescending, rude manner? In the following sentence, "pick up on" suffers from the same problems: "Tess failed to pick up on Alex d'Urbervilles' intentions." Does the writer mean that Tess didn't notice these intentions? That she didn't respond to them? That she said nothing about them? A final example (a statement about Tess and Angel Clare in Hardy's novel) combines a cliché with abstract terms and wordiness to create a pompous sentence: "The lack of communication factor created relationship problems and led to the deterioration of their marriage."

Preferring the Concrete to the Abstract

Abstract words, like *environment, justice, durability, age,* are necessary for thinking and writing. But they are often vague. Sentences with nothing but abstract words are often unintelligible.

Jonathan Swift's satiric irony in the first two books of *Gulliver's Travels* results from the juxtaposition of dimensional extremes that create differing perspectives. Largeness and smallness become antipodal means for envisioning the grossness and pettiness of existence.

Does the writer mean by "the juxtaposition of dimensional extremes" that Swift compares giants and pygmies? Using concrete words, the passage might be rewritten as follows:

Jonathan Swift's satiric irony in the first two books of *Gulliver's Travels* results from his comparison of extremely large and extremely small creatures. The Brobdingnagians illustrate the grossness of life, while the Lilliputians illustrate its pettiness.

SPECIAL PROBLEMS OF LITERARY PAPERS

The Author's Presence & the First-Person Pronoun

Should the author of a literary paper refer to himself or herself in the first person? Teachers of English disagree on this question. Professional critics often use the first person, as in the following passage from a Dickens scholar: "I may suggest in passing that the reason why Dickens used flat characters or label-characters, is twofold: He had a great many characters to handle and had to stamp them clearly and simply; he also wrote serially. . . . " Throughout the essay from which this sentence is quoted, the author again and again refers to himself in the first person. The alternatives to using the first person are often awkward: "One finds Dickens' minor characters to be predictable and stereotyped." Who is this "one"? If it is the author of the paper who finds the characters predictable and stereotyped, wouldn't it be preferable for him or her to say so by using the first-person pronoun? There are other evasions of the first-person pronoun nearly as awkward: "The reader of Dickens may find some of his characters excessively sentimental." Once again, if the view expressed belongs to the author of the paper, the first-person point of view and the first-person pronoun make more sense: "I find some of Dickens' characters excessively sentimental." The first-person pronoun holds the author responsible; it states clearly whose opinion is being advanced.

English teachers sometimes advise against the use of first-person references on the grounds that literary papers are formal essays, not informal personal essays. The distinction is valid; it points to the style and tone of formal essays, in which the author concentrates not on personal responses but on the subject at hand. As a general rule, keep yourself in the background of a formal literary essay. Furthermore, the phrases, "I think that," "I believe," "I feel," or "it is my opinion that" are often unnecessary. It is preferable to write, "Pip's ambition to become a gentleman causes him to leave his true friends," rather than, "I think that it is Pip's ambition to become a gentleman that causes him to leave his true friends." When it is clear that the words in the paper express the author's thoughts and feelings, the use of the first-person pronoun is redundant.

Avoiding References to "You"

Consider the use of the pronoun *you* in the following passage on Shakespeare's *Romeo and Juliet*: "The nurse is a gossipy old woman interested in the love life of the people around her, so you are not surprised when she recommends that Juliet marry Paris." The use of *you* makes the style inappropriately casual. The sentence revised without the *you* is preferable.

Using the Present Tense

Students often write about literature in the past tense: "Romeo suddenly **changed** his mind when he **attended** the Capulet's party and **saw** Juliet for the first time. He immediately **forgot** Rosaline and **fell** completely in love with Juliet." For most critical writing, use the present tense: "Romeo suddenly **changes** his mind when he **attends** the Capulet's party and **sees** Juliet for the first time." Literature exists in an eternal present. Assume that Romeo is forever falling in love with Juliet and that they are eternally being married by Friar Laurence.

Of course you need to use the past tense to discuss something prior to the events being discussed in the present tense: "When Romeo falls in love with Juliet, he immediately forgets Rosaline. He had earlier **told** his friends that he would never find a woman as beautiful as Rosaline."

Avoiding Verb Tense Shifts

Do not shift your verb tenses in a paper in such a way that you cause a shift in point of view:

When Romeo **attends** the Capulets' party he instantly **falls** in love with Juliet. He **forgot** Rosaline without a second thought. **Was** he being fickle? He **is** certainly changeable and very emotional.

This discussion, with its shifting verb tenses, causes disconcerting shifts in the point of view. In these sentences all verbs should be in the present tense.

Authors' Names

For male authors, give the full name when you first introduce the author: "In his autobiography, *Black Boy*, Richard Wright narrates the events of his early years." Exceptions: If the author is well-known (e.g., Dickens, Shakespeare, Sophocles), you may use the last name only.

After your first use of the name, refer to the author by his last name only (e.g., Richard Wright becomes Wright). Do not add a title (e.g., avoid references to Mr. Wright).

For women, convention traditionally dictated the full name throughout (e.g., Jane Austen, Emily Dickinson). Today, many writers treat women authors as they would males and refer to Austen or Dickinson after the first full use of the name.

Never use just the first name of an author, male or female.

Titles of Literary Works

For short works, use quotation marks for the title. This applies to short stories, poems, essays, chapters of books. On a typewriter or in pen, underline the titles of long works: <u>Hamlet</u>, <u>The Odyssey</u>. With a computer you can put titles of long works in italics, the convention that applies to printing: *Hamlet, The Odyssey*.

10

EDITING & REVISING

- Developing Editorial Skills
- The Tools of Editing
- Computer Editing Tools
- Peer Editing
- Questions for Editing
- The Editor at Work
- Revising on the Computer
- Proofreading

DEVELOPING EDITORIAL SKILLS

The Importance of Editing & Revising

Once you have turned out your final rough draft, plan to spend considerable time on editing and revising it. Revision is crucial for all writing, and editing is crucial for effective revising. Professional writers typically spend considerably more time editing and revising a draft than they do in creating it. The ability to create an effective literary composition of any sort depends as much on editing and revising as it does on creativity.

Good writers are good editors, a fact that is sometimes obscured by the image of writers as "creative." Understandably many students have not developed their editorial abilities, and often their creativity outpaces their editing. Signs of inadequate development of editorial skills are papers lively with bright ideas and valuable insights but lacking in coherence and thoroughness.

Editing as a Craft

Editors are made, not born. The skills that make a good editor can be learned. Fortunately everything you have been learning in your English classes—correct grammar, clear expression, proper diction—contributes to your development as an editor.

THE TOOLS OF EDITING

Desk Dictionary

Effective editing, like any craft, requires tools. The primary tool of an editor is a dictionary. You cannot begin to edit without a good dictionary, which means a complete hardbound desk dictionary in a recent edition. Do not rely on a paperback pocket dictionary, an abbreviated version handy to carry to class but not designed for the work you need to do when editing. Full-sized desk dictionaries have been prepared with students in mind, and they address many of the problems you confront when writing a paper. Most good desk dictionaries include discussions of grammar, usage, punctuation, and capitalization.

Grammar Handbook

Take your uncertainties about punctuation, capitalization, sentence mechanics, sentence structure, and correct grammar to a grammar handbook or composition handbook. Many grammar and writing guides provide sections on footnotes, endnotes, the preparation of a bibliography, and the writing of the research paper.

Thesaurus

A thesaurus can provide you with synonyms and help you to distinguish between the connotations of words. You can gain variety in your writing by using synonyms, and you can make distinctions in your argument when you know the subtle gradations in the meanings of synonyms. A thesaurus and a dictionary provide this kind of help. For example, which of the following words best describes the Hamlet we meet in Act 1: *moody, melancholy, melancholic, despairing, gloomy, depressed*? Why might the term *melancholy* be appropriate for Hamlet but not for Willie Loman in Arthur Miller's *Death of a Salesman*? Hamlet calls himself a *rogue* but uses the word *villain* for Claudius. What is the difference? Huck Finn might be called a *rogue* or a *rascal* but not a *villain* or a *scoundrel*. A thesaurus along with a dictionary provide word distinctions such a these.

Handbook to Literature

Handbooks or guides to literature define literary terms and concepts fully and provide commentary on literary periods and movements. While a dictionary can provide you with short definitions of terms such as *irony* or *metaphor*, a handbook will offer a full discussion with relevant examples.

COMPUTER EDITING TOOLS

Spelling Checker

If your writing program has this feature (and most do), it can run a spelling check on your document as part of your editing. Most spelling-checker programs not only flag incorrect spellings but also offer alternative spellings—a boon to those who cannot remember how to spell words like *occurrence*. For example, let us say you have mistakenly written the word *psychoanalisis* in your paper. The spelling checker will first flag the word as an unknown spelling. If you are uncertain how to correct your error, you ask the computer to suggest a correction. The spelling checker will suggest the correct spelling, *psychoanalysis,* and, if you request, will provide other words similar in spelling, such as *psychoanalyses, psychoanalysts,* and *psychoanalyst.*

Helpful as they are, computer spelling-checker programs do not solve all of your spelling problems. Most programs will not flag your confusions between *their, there,* and *they're,* nor tell you when you should use *principal* as opposed to *principle, except* rather than *accept.* These homonyms or sound-alike words present difficulties for computer programs, although some of the more recent style and grammar programs will flag instances of commonly confused homonyms to alert you to a possible error. However, the correct use of the word and the correct spelling is finally up to you, the author. In other words, despite computer technology there are still plenty of opportunities for you to make spelling errors and plenty of opportunities for you to use your printed dictionary and to learn correct spelling.

Computer Thesaurus

A computer thesaurus usually provides less than the printed version. If you ask it to suggest alternatives it provides a list of words, typically with no definitions. You are better off with the book.

Grammar & Style Checker

This computer feature can scan your document to point out your frequent (and thus possibly too-frequent) use of long sentences or repeated use of sentences with a certain construction, such as sentences using participles. Some programs flag fragments, incorrectly used adverbs and articles, and double negatives, among other errors. Some point out such potential problems as shifts in verb tenses and the references of pronouns. These programs can point out features of your writing that might be grammatically incorrect or stylistically awkward or repetitive, but they cannot do these things with any certainty. They must finally leave the choice of spelling, words, grammar, and style up to you. Most English teachers see these computer programs as limited. It continues to be the responsibility of authors to master English grammar and style; no machine has yet become a fine stylist in English or an effective teacher of style and grammar.

PEER EDITING

Your classmates can serve in far more valuable ways than any computer editing tools in helping you to write a clear paper. They can read and respond to your writing in ways difficult for you as author to do. Your classmates bring fresh eyes to the job. They can tell you if your writing makes sense to them. "I don't understand what you're trying to say in this paragraph," a classmate may say to you. "Your main idea confuses me." "Your thesis is not very clear," another classmate may tell you, "and I don't see that you've supported it convincingly." Although these are personal responses that require no formal training as an editor, they are among the most valuable responses you can receive as a writer. They alert you to aspects of your writing that need further work.

Your instructor may require you to submit your paper in draft to a classmate for review, or may give you the opportunity to work in class with your classmates, exchanging papers for editing. This exercise helps you as author by giving you an enlarged audience as well as fresh perspectives on your work. At the same time, your work in editing your classmates' papers helps to develop your editing skills.

If you are not assigned to do peer editing, ask your instructor if you may submit your paper to a classmate for review. If peer editing is not part of your course, be sure to gain permission for such work, because your instructor may consider such editing a form of plagiarism. If your instructor views your writing as homework that you should do on your own, he or she will consider peer editing inappropriate.

QUESTIONS FOR EDITING

Here is a list of questions that you might use for peer editing sessions or to ask of your own paper.

Content

Topic. Does the paper topic focus on something important in the work of literature? Is the topic too large for the paper? Is the topic focused?

Thesis. Is the thesis valid? Does it lead into the literature in helpful ways? Is the thesis clearly stated? Is the thesis adequately supported with specific examples and quotations from the texts?

The Essay as a Whole. Is the essay fully developed? Has the topic been covered thoroughly? Is the essay repetitive? Does it explain concepts clearly and define important terms? Does the essay moved forward in logical steps? Are there steps in the argument that should be rearranged? When you have finished the essay and reflect on it as a whole, does it seem clear and convincing? Are you left wondering about the author's thesis, conclusions, or focus?

Organization

Clear Plan. Is the essay coherent and logical in its overall organization? Does the essay need more planning?

Paragraphing. Are there enough paragraphs? Too many? Are the paragraph divisions logical? Is the sequence of paragraphs coherent? Are there fluent transitions between paragraphs? Does each paragraph advance a single important point? Are there paragraphs that serve as a grab-bag of diverse ideas and topics? Does each paragraph develop its topic fully? Does each paragraph support its main point with evidence and quotations?

Introduction

Does the introductory paragraph announce the topic clearly? Does it inform its readers of what works and authors will be discussed? Does it state the thesis? Does it suggest a plan of development that the essay will follow?

Conclusion

Does the final paragraph bring the essay to a close, or does the essay stop abruptly? Is the final paragraph merely repetition of conclusions stated clearly elsewhere? Does the final paragraph introduce a new idea that is not adequately developed?

Sentence Structure & Grammar

Can you find sentences that don't work—fragments, run-ons, other sentence structure problems? Are there problems with dangling participles? Can you find illogical shifts in verb tenses? Do the verbs agree with their subjects? Can you find pronoun problems, such as vague pronoun use or pronouns that lack an antecedent or fail to agree with their antecedent?

Style

Are there too many long sentences? Too many short, choppy sentences? Can you see ways to make the writing more fluent? More precise? Clearer? Are the word choices clear and correct? Does the level of diction—formal, informal, colloquial, slang—seem appropriate?

Strengths & Weaknesses

What are the chief strengths of the paper? Can you suggest ways for the writer to build on the strengths to create an even stronger paper? What are the chief weaknesses? What should the writer do to address these weaknesses?

The Sequence of Editing Tasks

The sequence of editing tasks outlined above moves you from large issues to progressively smaller and more refined tasks. Although you need not adhere rigidly to this sequence, you will find that it is based on the logic of beginning with major changes of major consequence. It would be a waste of time to polish the wording of a paragraph only to conclude later that the paragraph should be cut from the essay because it is irrelevant to the argument.

THE EDITOR AT WORK

Looking for Your Chronic Weaknesses

As an editor you should look especially closely for problems that have bothered you previously. Have you had trouble with the clear statement of your thesis? With repetition and wordiness? With a lack of focus? You develop your abilities as an editor if you analyze yourself as a writer, making a list of the kinds of errors that have undermined your recent papers.

Before editing your current paper, you might review your instructor's comments on your recent papers. Have you received back papers only to discover that several of what you thought were sentences have been labeled fragments? Have you written run-on or run-together sentences, or sentences with comma splices? Have teachers pointed out to you problems in the agreement of your subjects and verbs, or nouns and pronouns? Have you received comments on verb tense shifts? All of these are frequent trouble spots for students. Writing problems are often habitual. Work to know your chronic writing problems, then examine your paper closely with an eye to these problems. You may need to read your paper through once for each kind of error common to your writing—once just for spelling, for example, another time for verb tenses, a third time for pronoun problems.

Using correct grammar is in part a matter of habit. Writing, revising, editing, and rewriting papers provide excellent opportunities to develop correctness in language. Whenever you receive back a paper, whether or not your teacher has demanded that you rewrite it, you should turn to a grammar handbook and correct all of the errors in mechanics, wording, word choices, grammar, and sentence structure. You will be strengthening the editor in you, and you will be taking an important step in becoming a clear and correct writer.

Editing & Revising a Student Paper

The editor's work is illustrated in the editing and revising of the following student essay:

STUDENT PAPER ON RICHARD WRIGHT'S BLACK BOY

Richard Grows Up to Be a Writer

When Richard was growing up as a young boy he decided he wanted to be a writer. Writing was the means that he used to find a way to get out of the south and the white racist society he hated. His book shows how he learned about literature and writing and began to develop a writing career while he was still growing up in the south.

When he first learned about writing he was very young, right away, however he knew he wanted to learn more about it. A friend of his grandmother's, Ella read books and got Richard interested in literature. She read to him from a book she was reading and Richard is completely enchanted. The literature creates a whole imaginary world for him that he wants to live in.

> They could not have known that Ella's whispered story of deception and murder had been the first experience in my life that had elicited from me a total emotional response. No words of punishment could have possibly made me doubt. I had tasted what to me was life, and I would have more of it, somehow, someway. (48)

So even though he had to fight against the opposition of his family he becomes a writer. He writes an article for his newspaper called "The Voodoo of Hell's Half-Acre." That is the beginning of his life as a writer, and it causes more problems at home because his mother thinks he is wasting his time. He should be doing something more serious and successful. His aunt even thinks the story is sinful. He gets no support from his family. As usual he is a loner but this is part of his nature and the way he does almost everything.

Richard realizes he needs to go north to write. "I dreamed of going north and writing books, novels" (186). He knows that only if he gets away from his family and the south will he be able to write the way he wants without people telling him that blacks can't write or that writing is sinful and a waste of time.

Richard does some other work for a while, like learning to grind lenses, but he is unhappy with the work and he runs into white racists that make it impossible for him to work successfully. He knows he must become a writer and he knows he can only do this in the north. At the end he goes north where "life could be lived with dignity" and goes on to become one of the world's greatest writers.

The Essay's Virtues

Despite its errors and problems, this paper has something to say and a point of view. It is helpful to begin with the strengths of this paper, since its strong points can be developed. If you are uncertain where to begin in editing and revising, look first for a paper's virtues, since these form the valuable core on which revisions can be built.

Valuable Content

In the content area the strengths of this paper include an understanding that Richard's interest in literature has put him at odds with his family. However, this topic has not been fully articulated. A revision can bring it into clearer focus.

The paper has advanced a topic but has not stated a thesis clearly, although a thesis is implied by the argument. When asked to state this thesis more clearly, the student offered the following sentence: "Richard's love of literature and writing puts him in conflict with his family and finally drives him away from his family and the South so that he can pursue his dream of being a writer." This is a worthwhile thesis; it would help the paper if it were more clearly stated and more clearly argued. An important early step in revision would see that this thesis were more clearly stated in the essay and used to bring a clearer focus to the development.

Additional strengths include the way the second paragraph turns to Richard's enchantment with literature and accurately points out how it creates an imaginary world for the growing boy. In its final two paragraphs the paper shows the way that Richard's love of literature becomes part of his dream of escape from the South. The student has used some relevant quotations that bring into focus Richard's strong emotional response to literature. All of these aspects of the paper are valuable, and they make the paper worthy of further work.

Further work is certainly needed if this paper is to fulfill its promise. Although the student submitted it as a final draft—it was in fact his second draft—it has many of the problems of an early draft. It has promise, but the promise needs to be brought forth and articulated.

Revision of Content

Beginning with the content, an editor (which means in most cases the student author as his own editor) could point out several uncertainties and confusions and raise many questions, as follows:

Paragraph one. There's no mention of the work being discussed. The student should make clear from the beginning that this is a paper about a certain work of literature.

The writer refers to a time "when Richard was growing up," which is too vague. When did the boy learn about literature? When did he begin to develop a writing career? The paragraph implies that he began to develop a writing career when he was a young boy. Doesn't it really want to say that as a boy Richard began to show an interest in literature and that this interest would later blossom into a dream of a writing career?

Paragraph two. The paper says that Richard learned about writing when he was very young, but doesn't this statement confuse his first experience of hearing a story with his first experience of writing? If the student were to turn to the section of the autobiography from which he quoted, he would discover that it concerns Richard's *listening* to a story, not his reading of literature nor his own writing. The confusion of Richard's love of literature and his interest in becoming a writer, which surfaces in this paragraph, weakens the entire paper. An interest in reading literature and an interest in writing it are not identical, yet this paper talks about them as if they were.

Paragraph three. The discussion of Richard's first efforts at writing is undeveloped. The author needs to say more on this topic. What did the writing mean to Richard? What was this article he wrote? Wouldn't the opposition of the family be clearer if it were more fully delineated?

Paragraph four. Richard's dream of going north is tied to his dream of writing in an unclear way. Why can't he write in the South?

Paragraph five. Should this discussion of "other work" be a part of this paper? Does it contribute to the thesis? Doesn't it distract our attention from the topic of Richard's growing dream of becoming a writer? The idea that Richard must go north to write is repeated with little change in wording and no development from its statement in paragraph four. Paragraph five ends with a judgment that is not relevant to the thesis and makes readers wonder on what authority the student calls Richard Wright "one of the world's greatest writers." (This is not to deny greatness to Wright but to point out that judgments about greatness are not convincing or helpful in a paper of this sort.) The writer should question whether paragraph five adds anything valuable to the paper. Possibly the writer can come up with a new final paragraph, or he might find ways to develop the fourth paragraph so that it can serve as a conclusion.

The work as a whole. An editor could point out to the author that the essay needs a clearer statement of thesis and a clearer, more logical development of the argument. Like many student papers, this one needs enlargement. Only by enlarging on Richard's dreams and on the stages of his growth will the paper become clear, illustrating the way clarity is often dependent on the full development of an argument. The paper in its present draft is sketchy and tentative and rushes over points that need more attention. It is a puzzling and frustrating paper to read.

Revision of Organization

An editor can approve of the way the paper moves from stages early in Richard's childhood to the final stages of his growing up. The repetition in the last two paragraphs points to the need for a clearer ending and possibly a new final paragraph.

Revision of Sentence Structure, Grammar, & Mechanics

Fundamental errors in sentence structure and grammar leap from the page and create the impression of an author writing carelessly. The paper needs numerous revisions, but it is helpful to remember that the need for some of these revisions might be removed by content changes. Here are some of the more obvious errors and problems:

- The verb tenses shift from past to present in paragraph two. The shift in verb tenses divides the essay into two perspectives. At first the author of the paper writes from the perspective of the past, which says that these events in Richard's life are over and finished. This is the perspective of the autobiography, and, since Wright works from this retrospective point of view, looking back at a past that is finished, the past tense works as well for a paper discussing the book. On the other hand, writing about literature generally uses the present tense, making the assumption that in the realm of the imagination the action presented by a novel, poem, or play occurs in the eternal present. In this case the literature is nonfiction, so the author of the paper can more easily capture the perspective of the autobiography by using the past. In any case, the author must be consistent; whichever tense he uses should run throughout the entire paper.
- The first sentence of paragraph two runs together two independent clauses with a comma (comma splice) and incorrectly punctuates the word *however*. Here are four possible revisions:

  1. Revision with a semicolon: "When he first learned about writing he was very young; right away, however, he knew he wanted to learn more about it."
  2. Revision into two sentences: "When he first learned about writing he was very young. Right away, however, he knew he wanted to learn more about it."
  3. Revision with coordinating conjunction: "When he first learned about writing he was very young, but right away he knew he wanted to learn more about it."

4. Revision using subordination (an initial dependent or subordinate clause followed by an independent clause): "Although he was very young when he first learned about writing, he knew at once he wanted to learn more about it."

• The word *South* should be capitalized when it is used as the name of a region.

• In paragraph two, the possessive, "a friend of his grandmother's, Ella" is an error, since the relationship is already shown by the preposition *of*. Without the apostrophe, however, the wording becomes ambiguous—"a friend of my grandmother, Ella"—which causes us to wonder if Ella may not be the name of the grandmother. The absence of a comma after the name, Ella, is an error and creates confusion. A simple revision resolves these difficulties: "Ella, a friend of his grandmother, awakened Richard's interest in literature when. . . . " This obviously edits and revises the wording in other ways as well: it removes *got*, which is awkward and colloquial, and substitutes the verb *awakens*.

Revision of Word Choice & Style

The essay lacks sophistication and polish. It is often repetitive and wordy. Here are some examples:

• The first sentence includes redundant wording, "growing up as a young boy." "As a young boy" should be cut from the sentence. However, there is little point in fussing with this sentence until the paragraph has been rewritten to clarify the content.

• The second sentence is wordy and repetitive. It should be stated more succinctly. Here is a sample revision: "He used writing to escape from the South and the white racist society he hated." This revision yields a saving of nine words.

• The indented quotation begins with the pronoun "they," which lacks a noun for reference in the paper. The author needs to introduce the quotation so that the antecedent of *they* is clear, or else omit the first six words of the quotation.

• Paragraph three opens with wordiness: "So even though he had to fight against the opposition of his family. . . ." A possible revision: "Despite the opposition of his family, he became a writer."

• There are inadequate transitions linking the paragraphs, especially at the beginnings of paragraphs three and four.

• The verb *gets* is overused and badly used: "He gets no support from his family" might be changed to, "He received no support from his family." "He knows that only if he gets away from his family . . ." can be changed to, "He knew that only if he escaped his family. . . ." The verb *knows* or its past tense *knew* are not the best choice; instead, the sentence would reflect Richard's state of mind more accurately if it stated, "He *believed* that only if he escaped his family. . . ."

• Many sentences can be reworded more succinctly with a gain in fluency and ease.

The Need for Deep Revision

The above suggestions for revision are many and extensive. They demand considerable work. Editing of early drafts typically calls for such deep and extensive revision. In other words, true editing and revising dig deep. Many students balk at the process. They often feel that once they have written the draft they consider final, major revisions should not be demanded. If only this were the case! Professional writers teach us otherwise; revisions must often be more like major surgery than cosmetic care. Only at the final stages is editing a matter of proofreading for spelling and minor errors and the polishing that substitutes one slightly better word for another.

The student author of the paper on Wright found that he needed two more drafts and a conference with his teacher before he finally wrote the paper that fulfilled the promise of the early draft and pleased him and his teacher. The student was fortunate in having access to a computer and having the paper on a computer file, making the extensive revisions far easier than they would have been if he had worked on them at a typewriter or with pen and ink. His use of a computer for these revisions is outlined in the next section.

REVISING ON THE COMPUTER

Editing & Revising at the Computer Keyboard

Nowhere do the virtues of computers as word processors shine more clearly than in revisions of written documents. Here are the steps of revising on a computer as illustrated by the student's revisions of the paper on Richard Wright. Students without access to a computer can use the same steps with pen and paper or a typewriter, although the steps will take more time.

Using Printed Copy

In addition to editing on the screen, the student edited and revised on the page by printing out his edited versions so that he might work on them with pen or pencil. Most professional writers who use a computer for their writing find that both kinds of editing are essential. First you edit text on the screen at the keyboard, then when you have made all of the changes you feel are needed you print the document to edit on the page, where you will most likely find still more problems and errors.

Cutting & Saving Text

The student decided that he would remove his final paragraph altogether. To do this, he might have selected the entire paragraph and then hit the delete key. However, he wanted to save the paragraph since he felt he might use sentences or phrases from it in his revised version. Thus he cut the paragraph and saved it in a scrapbook.

Perhaps the easiest way to save an early draft is to leave it in its entirety in the file, either at the beginning or at the end of the document. In this way the author can turn to it at any time, copy it paragraph by paragraph for editing work, and take phrases or sentences from it for a final draft.

Cutting, Moving, & Pasting Text

In revising his paper, the student decided to use the third sentence in the opening paragraph as the first sentence. Here's the first paragraph in the original:

> When Richard was growing up as a young boy he decided he wanted to be a writer. Writing was the means that he used to find a way to get out of the south and the white racist society he hated. His book shows how he learned about literature and writing and began to develop a writing career while he was still growing up in the south.

The student selected the last sentence and used the edit command to cut. This removed the sentence from the paragraph and saved it in the clipboard. Then he positioned the cursor at the beginning of the first sentence and used the editing command to paste the sentence into his document. It reappeared as the first sentence as follows (the cut-and-pasted sentence in bold):

> **His book shows how he learned about literature and writing and began to develop a writing career while he was still growing up in the south.** When Richard was growing up as a young boy he decided he wanted to be a writer. Writing was the means that he used to find a way to get out of the south and the white racist society he hated.

This cut and paste operation is just the first step in revising the opening paragraph. To work well as an opening, the paragraph needs sentence revisions.

Revising Text

First the student deleted the words, "His book," without saving them. With the cursor at the beginning of the paragraph, he typed, "In his autobiography, Black Boy, Richard Wright" so that the sentence now opens the paragraph with a reference to the literature under discussion: "In his autobiography, Black Boy, Richard Wright shows how he learned about literature and writing and began to develop a writing career while he was still growing up in the south."

Next the student deleted the two sentences that followed the new first sentence so that he could combine the opening sentence with the second paragraph. The new paragraph reads as follows:

In his autobiography, Black Boy, Richard Wright shows how he learned about literature and writing and began to develop a writing career while he was still growing up in the south. When he first learned about writing he was very young, right away, however he knew he wanted to learn more about it. A friend of his grandmother's, Ella read books and got Richard interested in literature. She read to him from a book she was reading and Richard is completely enchanted. The literature creates a whole imaginary world for him that he wants to live in.

The student now has a new opening paragraph, one that moves more quickly than did the original to discuss a specific example of Richard learning about literature. The paragraph still has some of the content, grammar, and word choice problems of the first draft, but the student has begun the task of major revision by moving text and creating a potentially better opening.

Adding Words & Phrases to the Text

To add words to his first sentence, the student positioned the cursor after the word *how* and before *he* to type the additional words, "as a very young boy," indicating more clearly when in Richard's life the event occurred. The student added other phrases by positioning the cursor, so that the enlarged first sentence reads as follows, with the additions printed in bold:

In his autobiography, Black Boy, Richard Wright shows how, **as a very young boy**, he learned about **the seductive power of** literature and writing and began to develop **an interest in** a writing career while he was still growing up in the south.

The addition of the phrase, "the seductive power of," adds emphasis to the sentence and more fully expresses the pull that the young boy felt in listening to the story of Bluebeard. The third addition, "an interest in," refines the idea of Richard's developing a writing career.

Correcting Grammar, Sentence Structure, & Mechanics

Working directly on the text on the screen, the student deleted errors such as the lower-case "s" in *south* and cut completely the sentence with the comma splice (the second sentence in the revised paragraph) and the faulty punctuation of *however*. He rewrote the sentence that introduces his stay with his grandmother and his listening to the story of Bluebeard. Notice in the revision that the student has changed not only grammar but also content; in the revision we learn that Ella had not read him but told him the story. The distinction between reading and telling a story may seem like a small point, but it is one made by Wright, and the student's paper is more precise and accurate with the revision.

Creating New Text

Notice in the revised version that the student has created additional text in keeping with the demand for greater development. He has added commentary plus a long, indented quotation. In addition, the student has added a second paragraph to comment on the quotation, thus further developing his paper and showing that this first experience of hearing a story served as a basis for Richard's later vocation as a writer. In this way the student has explored his topic in greater depth.

REVISED STUDENT PARAGRAPHS

In his autobiography, *Black Boy,* Richard Wright shows how, as a very young boy, he learned about the seductive power of literature and began to develop an interest in a writing career while growing up in the South. When he stayed with his grandmother, he often observed Ella, a schoolteacher who boarded with his grandmother, reading books. He asked her to read to him. She told him the story of Bluebeard. Right away Richard was completely enchanted. The literature created a whole imaginary world for him that he wanted to live in.

> The tale made the world around me be, throb, live. As she spoke, reality changed, the look of things altered, and the world became peopled with magical presences. My sense of life deepened and the feel of things was different, somehow. Enchanted and enthralled, I stopped her constantly to ask for details. My imagination blazed. The sensations the story aroused in me were never to leave me. (47)

These words show how important literature was to become in Richard's life. They reveal the basis for his future career as a writer. Unfortunately, Richard's grandmother and mother disapproved of his listening to the story, because they believed stories were "the Devil's work" (48). "They could not have known that Ella's whispered story of deception and murder had been the first experience in my life that had elicited from me a total emotional response" (48). This was the beginning of the opposition in Richard's life between his love of literature and his family's view that it was sinful and a waste of time.

This revision creates a thoroughly new second paragraph incorporating a quotation that in the first draft was indented but now is run on into the student's text. Since the quotation is a single sentence and takes fewer than three lines of the student's paper, it is better run on in this way. Notice that now the nouns *grandmother* and *mother* serve as antecedents for the pronoun *they* that begins the quotation. In this way the student has successfully blended his text with the quotation, whereas previously the pronoun lacked an antecedent.

The new second paragraph makes clear the opposition of Richard and his family over the issue of literature. The student had stated that this was his chief topic, but he had failed to bring it into clear focus in the original, so the greater clarity in the revision marks a large improvement.

Here is the entire essay in its final revision. You can gain some sense of what steps the student took to come up this revision by comparing it paragraph by paragraph and sentence by sentence with the very first draft.

REVISED STUDENT PAPER ON RICHARD WRIGHT'S BLACK BOY

Richard Grows Up to Be a Writer

In his autobiography, *Black Boy,* Richard Wright shows how, as a very young boy, he learned about the seductive power of literature and began to develop an interest in a writing career while growing up in the South. When he stayed with his grandmother, he often observed Ella, a schoolteacher who boarded with his grandmother, reading books. He asked her to read to him. She told him the story of Bluebeard. Right away Richard was completely enchanted. The literature created a whole imaginary world for him that he wanted to live in.

> The tale made the world around me be, throb, live. As she spoke, reality changed, the look of things altered, and the world became peopled with magical presences. My sense of life deepened and the feel of things was different, somehow. Enchanted and enthralled, I stopped her constantly to ask for details. My imagination blazed. The sensations the story aroused in me were never to leave me. (47)

These words show how important literature was to become in Richard's life. They reveal the basis for his future career as a writer. Unfortunately, Richard's grandmother and mother disapproved of his listening to the story, because they believed stories were "the Devil's work" (48). "They could not have known that Ella's whispered story of deception and murder had been the first experience in my life that had elicited from me a total emotional response" (48). This was the beginning of the opposition in Richard's life between his love of literature and his family's view that it was sinful and a waste of time.

When Richard came to write his first story, "The Voodoo of Hell's Half-Acre," published in a local newspaper, this opposition of his family became more pronounced. His Uncle Tom said the story had "no point" (185), and his

Aunt Addie "said that it was a sin for anyone to use the word hell" (185). His grandmother called the story "the Devil's work" (185), and his mother thought that writing showed that Richard was "weak-minded" (185). So Richard found no encouragement at home. This lack of encouragement typified his life at that time, because his family showed little support for anything he did or said.

Without any encouragement from his family, Richard believed he had to escape his home and the South in order to write. He needed to go north. "I dreamed of going north and writing books, novels" (186). The North became for him an imaginary land "where everything was possible." He felt the same lack of encouragement from the racist white society in the South as he felt from his family. "I was building up in me a dream which the entire educational system of the South had been rigged to stifle" (186). At this time he was only 15 years old, but he felt certain he must leave the South if he was to succeed as a writer.

Richard Wright brought his autobiography to a close with his leaving the South and taking a train north. He hoped that in the North life could be lived with dignity, something that was always denied him by the racist South and even by his family. "I was leaving without a qualm, without a single backward glance" (281). As he traveled north he recalled his reading of literature as the motivating force in his life. "It had been my accidental reading of fiction and literary criticism that had evoked in me vague glimpses of life's possibilities" (283). From his early years in the South to this departure for the North, literature was the most important influence in developing Richard Wright's life and career.

Looking closely at this revision, you see that the work the student put in was more fundamental than mere proofreading or fussing with mechanics. The improvement in the paper rests on its enlargement and development of the topic. The final version has about 140 words more than the original draft, but more important than greater length is greater focus and clarity. The sharper focus includes cutting repetitions and unneeded words (e.g., the material on Richard's job grinding lenses) as well as adding commentary and quotations. It is worth noting how dense with quotations the final version has become, bringing the reader into much closer contact with the work under discussion.

PROOFREADING

The Final Step

Before you submit your paper, read it closely one last time for mechanical errors (e.g., errors in spelling, punctuation, the use of the apostrophe). If you are using a computer, do your proofreading on printed copy. It is often difficult to see errors in mechanics on the screen.

Proofreading on a computer can be done before the final formatting. For example, you might proofread your paper in a typeface such as Geneva that is large and clear but then put your paper into a different typeface before printing its final copy. For similar reasons you might use a larger type size—14 or even 18 point—or triple spacing as you work on the text but change to a smaller size (10 or 12 point usually) and double spacing for the final printing.

11

FORMATTING

- **Formatting as the Final Step**
- **Formatting on a Computer**
- **Manuscript Conventions**

FORMATTING AS THE FINAL STEP

When you have completed your final editing, you are ready to put your paper in its final form, or format. The word *format* refers to the layout of a publication or paper, the size and appearance of the paper used, the placement of the title, the typefaces, spacing of lines, and other aspects of appearance and form.

Look on the format as the final dressing you give to your paper. Although format is not as important as your ideas and conclusions, it produces an immediate impact on your reader and can weigh heavily in an evaluation of the worth of your paper. Imagine two papers with identical content, but with paper X carefully prepared on a typewriter or computer, paper Y carelessly handwritten on poor quality paper with many cross-outs and sloppily written corrections. Is it any surprise that paper X earns the higher grade?

FORMATTING ON A COMPUTER

With the increasing use of computers, more and more students understand the significance of format. Formatting is a category of computer tasks that includes commands for moving and shaping text, selecting the size and look of the typeface or font, setting the margins, and inserting borders and enclosing boxes, among other functions.

With a computer, writers commonly save the final formatting until the end. Typically, formatting forms the concluding step before printing out the finished paper. (On a typewriter you obviously need to set up your format as you begin typing your final draft.)

Computers allow you to choose one format for working on the screen and another for printing out your final copy. For example, you might use a large typeface (called a *font* in many computer programs) and triple spacing for clarity on the screen while you work, then shift to a smaller type face and double spacing. Some typefaces are clearer on the screen, such as Geneva (used here for illustration) because they lack *serifs*, a fine line finishing off the main strokes at the top or bottom. Thus you might select Geneva for your work on the screen but another typeface with serifs for your final formatting.

Paper

Use 8 1/2 x 11-inch paper with clean edges. Use white typing paper or composition paper, not paper torn from a spiral notebook. If you use computer paper, separate the sheets and trim the track-feed margins before submitting the work. For years it has been the convention to use only one side of the paper when preparing a manuscript; concerns for protecting the environment and saving paper have encouraged teachers and students to use both sides.

Typeface

If you write by hand, use black or dark blue ink. If you type, use a black ribbon. If you use a computer, you may have several typefaces available to you in different sizes and in different styles. It is best to use standard typefaces (e.g., Geneva, New York, Courier, Palatino) in standard sizes, such as 12 point (the size of these letters). Save the unusual or dramatic typefaces for your creative and personal writing. Standard styles are less intrusive and serve you better in a paper on literature, though there are several important uses for *italics* and **bold face.**

MANUSCRIPT CONVENTIONS

Double Spacing

Since your papers are manuscripts (as opposed to printed or published material), you should use double spacing, which allows space between the lines for comments and corrections. Your peer editors and teacher need this space for comments and corrections.

Titles

All papers, no matter how brief, need titles. For a long paper such as a thesis, you need a separate title page. Few of the papers you write in your English courses require a separate title page unless your teacher asks for one.

Center your title two or three inches from the top of the first page of your writing. On ruled paper write the title on the top line, then leave a space before beginning your paper. For a paper written on a typewriter or computer, the space between the title and your first paragraph should be greater than the space between your lines of text.

You may put the title in bold face or in type sizes larger than the rest of your text. Do *not* use quotation marks or underlining for your title, since these indicate a published work. For the same reason avoid putting your title in italics. Of course if you include the title of a published work in your title, you need to use quotation marks around the title of a short work and underlining or italics for the title of a long work. Compare the following paper titles as examples of how to indicate titles and quotations from literary works. Notice that all of these paper titles are centered on the page.

The Character of Hamlet

A Study of Shakespeare's *Hamlet*

An Analysis of Hamlet's "To be or not to be" Soliloquy

Poetic Imagery in Frost's "Nothing Gold Can Stay"

Student's Name, Course Identification, Date

This information goes on a separate title page if you are using one, or on the first page in the upper left or upper right corner. Consult your teacher on the preferred form, the information to include, and the proper placement.

Margins

Top and bottom margins. One inch. This is the default (preset) top and bottom margin for many word-processing programs. If you use such a program, you needn't make any changes.

Side margins. An inch and a quarter on each side (the default setting on many computer programs) or an inch and a half on the left and an inch or inch and a quarter on the right. On student papers (and on all manuscripts), margins serve as space for comments and corrections as well as for appearance.

Numbering

Number all of your pages except your title page and first page with Arabic numerals. Standard manuscript conventions call for the number at the upper right corner of the page, although it may also appear at the lower right or centered at top or bottom.

Many computer programs allow you to put a number icon into your header or footer and let the program number the pages in sequence automatically.

Justifying the Margins

A margin is said to be justified when it is flush or even, as are the left and right margins on this page. With a computer it is easy to justify both margins in the style of a printed book. Standard manuscript conventions call for the left margin to be justified and the right margin ragged (uneven), the preferred form for papers on literature. If you like experimenting with different appearances for your paper, such as margin justification, do this on other kinds of writing.

Paragraphing

Indent the first line of each paragraph five spaces. Do not leave spaces between paragraphs.

Setting Up Quotations of Prose

If you quote less than three lines of prose, put quotation marks around the quoted material and run it on double spaced in the body of your text. If you quote three or more lines of prose, set the quoted material apart single spaced with the left margin three or more spaces wider than your regular margin. Indented quotations of prose should be typed with the left margin justified. The single spacing and wider margin tell your reader at a glance that this is quoted material, and for this reason you do not use quotation marks, except where they occur in the original material. Indented quotations are often introduced by a colon. Consult the sample quotations throughout this guide.

Setting Up Quotations of Verse

When you quote one, two, or three lines of poetry, run them on in your text with quotation marks. Use a slash to indicate the end of a line, as in this quotation from Robert Frost: "Two roads diverged in a yellow wood,/And sorry I could not travel both / And be one traveler." Longer quotations should be single spaced and written as they appear in the original without quotation marks. Follow the author's pattern of stanzas, indentation, punctuation, and so forth. Here, for example, is the first stanza of Robert Herrick's "To the Virgins, to Make Much of Time," set up correctly:

> Gather ye rosebuds while ye may,
> Old Time is still a-flying;
> And this same flower that smiles today
> Tomorrow will be dying.

Notice that while the quoted verse is indented beyond the paragraph indent of the text, the lines are not centered but run with a left-justified margin. Sometimes students using computers prefer to center poetry. If this were done with the quotation from Herrick, it would look like this:

> Gather ye rosebuds while ye may,
> Old Time is still a-flying;
> And this same flower that smiles today
> Tomorrow will be dying.

This formatting is correct if it resembles the formatting on the original page. It is not correct for lines of prose, which should be quoted with the left margin justified.

PLANNING IN ACTION
Visions and Realities in a Country Town

Small towns in rural areas are recognised by the Office of Population Censuses and Surveys as likely to be the main growth areas in the next decade. This study charts the expansion of one such town, Honiton in East Devon, over the years 1964 to 1980; a period during which its civilian population grew by nearly two-thirds, and it was the focus of considerable planning interest. The study examines the relationship between three aspects of the planning process: the selection of political goals, the delivery of statutory services and the designation of land use. It explores the dynamics of change, both in what was happening and in what was sought, and in so doing seeks to delineate the limits of the possible.

Anne Glyn-Jones is Research Fellow in the Department of Geography at the University of Exeter. Her previous publications include *Growing Older in a South Devon Town* (University of Exeter 1975 – out of print); *Village into Town. A Study of Transition in South Devon.* (University of Exeter and Devon County Council 1977 – out of print); *(Rural Recovery: Has it Begun?* (University of Exeter and Devon County Council 1979) and *Small Firms in a Country Town* (University of Exeter and Devon County Council 1982).

£3.50 net   ISBN 0 85989 169 0

Devon County Council and the University of Exeter